The Fountainheadache

THE FOUNTAINHEADACHE

THE POLITICS OF
ARCHITECT–CLIENT RELATIONS

Andy Pressman

JOHN WILEY & SONS, INC.
New York   Chichester   Brisbane   Toronto   Singapore

Also by Andy Pressman
Architecture 101: A Guide to the Design Studio

Library of Congress Cataloging in Publication Data:

Pressman, Andy.
    The fountainheadache : the politics of architect-client relations
/ Andy Pressman.
      p.   cm.
Includes index.
ISBN 0-471-30992-3 (pbk. : alk. paper)
    1. Architects and patrons—United States.   2. Architectural
practice—United States—Management.   I. Title.
NA1996.P75   1995
720'.68–dc20   94-40081

Printed in the United States of America

10 9 8 7 6 5 4 3 2 1

TO ALL MY CLIENTS
FOR THEIR FAITH AND INSPIRATION

FOREWORD

This book is long overdue, and if it reaches its intended audiences it has the potential of building a bridge across the gap that frequently separates architect and client. All too often when this chasm is present, what should be a joyfully creative process bogs down in frustration and failed expectations.

Philadelphia architect Vincent G. Kling FAIA, one of a half-dozen peers[1] who built large, successful, award-winning firms in the 1960s out of a combination of architectural talent and extraordinary skill at communicating with clients, once observed:

> No architect, no matter how good, can do a good building for a bad client. Conversely, no architect, no matter how bad, can do a truly bad building for a good client.

He went on to add: "There is no such thing as an architect alone on a desert island," for without a client there can be no architect. This is the first and fundamental element that clients and architects all too often forget. If anything worthwhile is going to come of an engagement between client and architect, they must see their roles as inseparable.

---

1. For example: William Periera, John Carl Warnecke, Welton Beckett, Victor Gruen, Charles Luckman, and so on.

The legal concept of "agency" gives social standing to the relationship. The architect, as a professional, is different from the vendor, supplier, contractor, or other businesses that are part of the building process. As a professional, the architect is agent for the client—legally an authorized extension of the client— and obligated to put the clients' interest above self-interest.

Thus, when an architect and client first meet to undertake a project they are supposed to become as one. But this happens only when both parties are able to communicate in a manner that this book tries to illustrate: A manner in which the client has full trust that the architect understands and is representing the client's interests above all else, and the architect can trust the client to be dealing from a full and open deck. When this type of relationship occurs, the results are memorable. Making it happen, however, takes some practice. Here are a few illustrations that may point the way.

New Jersey architect Herman Hassinger, FAIA, whose practice is heavily involved with churches, one of the more notoriously difficult clients since it is inevitably represented by a diverse committee, says he begins all his interviews with prospective church clients with this warning:

> You must be aware that, despite whatever your and my best intentions may be, there are three absolute rules of human enterprise:
>
> ❖ Nothing is as simple as you thought it would be.
>
> ❖ Nothing goes as quick as you thought it would go.
>
> ❖ Nothing ever ends up costing what you expected to spend.
>
> That's true for remodeling the kitchen, your daughter's wedding, and building a church.

He also tells them that if they accept these rules, the results will usually exceed their fondest hopes.

Stuart Furman, a professor of architecture at New York Institute of Technology, who maintains a small private practice in Brooklyn, New York, says he breaks the ice with all new clients this way:

> I tell them the process will be like a three-act play: The first act will get us all excited, but there is always a second act when it will look like it has all fallen apart. At the lowest point everyone may

be on the verge of giving up and abandoning the effort. There is always this low point—the client can't agree on changes to the program; the cost has gotten too high; the contractor reads the documents wrong and there is a fight over who will pay; and so on. Only if we forewarn the client can they have the fortitude to see it through to the final curtain—when the result becomes worth all the effort.

This writer's observation is that the single most important place to test and hopefully cement the best client–architect relationships is in the development of the program—before any sketches or images are discussed. From the architect's standpoint the ideal program is a statement of functions, and what responses or behaviors should occur around those functions. For example, "the living room needs to seat six for intimate conversation," "the kitchen should have lots of natural light and views of the garden," "the master bedroom needs to be in the quietest part of the house (or closest to the nursery)," and so on. Where program statements most often go astray are when clients say things like "I want it to look Colonial," or "I don't want it to be brick," and so on. There is a time for discussion of images and materials, but it is best deferred until after the plan has accommodated the program.

A partner of California architect Frank Gehry, one of the most avant-garde image-makers of the 1980s and 1990s, reports that Gehry never shows images or elevations to clients until after the plan is completely presented, understood, and accepted. "If the client is persuaded the building is going to work," said Gehry's partner, "they almost never question what Frank is doing with the exterior design."

One of the most frequent misunderstandings that sour architect–client communication is over the definition of "architecture" itself. The writer once was asked to advise the building committee of a small city library on how to select an architect for an expansion. The committee included both a builder and an engineer who were offering considerable advice, from their perspectives, about how it could be done most expeditiously and economically. The writer advised:

The first thing you need to decide is whether you want this addition to be just a building or whether you would like the result to be architecture.

After a little discussion to be sure everyone understood the implications of the difference, the committee retired to executive session and quickly voted, unanimously, that they wanted architecture.

They were a good client, they chose a young but promising architect, and together they produced architecture.

May this book help many others do the same.

WELD COXE

PREFACE

This vivid triumphal image (Figure 1) from the classic film adaptation of Ayn Rand's *The Fountainhead* runs through the imagination of many architects as they struggle to resolve personal ideals with the realities of professional practice. *The Fountainheadache* sets forth many of the potentials and problems of architect–client relations, involving many types of projects and firms working in an era of tight budgets and wary consumers.

The plight of both architects and their clients in today's residential, commercial, and institutional settings is the theme of *The Fountainheadache*. The goal of the book is to serve as a wake-up call to both architects and clients. The message is that much of the difficulty between architects and clients is political, and that projects are unsuccessful when communication fails and the consequent struggles for control are not fully resolved. In other words, it is the quality of the evolving *personal relationships* between the key parties that is of utmost importance. Personal and professional style may vary greatly, but the one constant in truly successful projects seems to be defined by indelibly etched architect–client relationships.

The Fountainheadache speaks to the array of forces shaping projects and the relationships driven by those forces. The strength of this book is due in large part to the quality and insights of the remarkable group of contributors, many of whom are world-renowned architects. Narratives, interviews, and ac-

FIGURE 1
A fresh breeze off New York Harbor ruffled through Patricia Neal's hair. She rose higher and higher, riding the makeshift elevator toward the very top of the almost-complete skyscraper. At the top stood Gary Cooper, adding more height and strength to the unfinished building. Shoulder-to-shoulder with the construction crew, he surveyed his creation and his domain. Photo © 1949 Turner Entertainment Co. All Rights Reserved. Still from the movie The Fountainhead, *courtesy of George Eastman House.*

companying visuals describe over 25 projects representing and defining successful and unsuccessful outcomes. There is broad hilarity and there is bitter disappointment. There are instances in which the client is thrilled, but the architect is barely able to accept his commission. There are cases when the architect is elated and the client is outraged. Finally, there are those special projects in which all manner of colliding values, agendas, expectations, and constraints are somehow resolved and lead to optimal service, good architecture, and satisfaction for all.

As a mosaic of people and projects reexamined, *The Fountainheadache* is really a collective memoir—one that I hope will promote interest among those who have even a passing flirtation with architecture as well as among clients of architects, and of course the design professionals themselves. I believe that professional development and public education converge where architects and clients interact to produce excellence in the built environment. This book is intended to promote such interaction through its focus on more effective and gratifying politics between architect and client.

ANDY PRESSMAN, AIA

Cambridge, Massachusetts
August, 1994

ACKNOWLEDGMENTS

Much appreciation and respect are extended to the editors at Wiley: Everett Smethurst, Linda Bathgate, Amanda Miller, and Diana Cisek.

I am grateful to the contributors who are largely responsible for the depth and high quality of material in *The Fountainhead-ache* (in alphabetical order): Stanley Allan, Thomas Bakalars, Carol Ross Barney, Marvin Cantor, Weld Coxe, Duo Dickinson, Jeremiah Eck, Robert Greenstreet, Charles Gwathmey, George Hartman, Eugene Kohn, William Lam, Kent Larson, Roger Lewis, William Kirby Lockard, Charles McAfee, Charles Moore, Douglas Oliver, Joseph Provey, Norman Rosenfeld, Renate Schweiger, John Seiler, Gary Siebein, Cathy Simon, James Stageberg, Stanley Tigerman, Susan Allen Toth, and Jack Travis.

The following individuals deserve special mention:

* Edward Allen for his continuing support.

* Stuart Ng at Warner Brothers Archives at the School of Cinema—Television at the University of Southern California for his assistance and patience in compiling stills from *The Fountainhead*.

* Kevin Keim at Moore/Andersson Architects for his responsiveness.

❖ Sue Gowans, without whom this book would have been completed much sooner, and for providing creative inspiration.

❖ Peter Pressman, Eleanor Pressman, and Iris Slikerman as always.

Qualifying Note

All the stories in *The Fountainheadache* are true. However, identifying circumstances for some projects have been changed to maintain client anonymity.

CONTENTS

The Fountainheadache

CHAPTER 1

DOMESTIC AFFAIRS

Clients in the residential domain are generally perceived by architects as the most puzzling. Design input and criticism by clients of proposed schemes often *seem* irrational and contradictory. Decisions may be delayed, and, worse, frequently changed even after the project is well into construction. On the other hand, residential clients may justly feel intimidated, as their needs and preferences are ignored by architects. This problem may be amplified since many architects view house design as fertile ground for aesthetic experimentation—pushing the design envelope. Communication may break down, and any feelings of mutual trust and respect—so essential to successful projects—disappear.

Typically, it is the small-size architectural firm that dominates the field in tackling the design of residential additions, renovations, or completely new construction. This small firm is often composed of young architects who are attempting to break-out on their own and establish a practice. Profit margins are usually very low, with projects quite time-intensive. However, there is an intrinsic payback: Independence, control (within the firm), and pride of authorship—from inception through construction.

Again there is potential for conflict since clients have a tendency to view young practitioners either as inexperienced or uninterested in the more technical aspects of projects. Suzanne Stephens, a noted architectural critic and editor, has said,

When it comes to the mundane matters of temperature, noise, and the like, there is always the lurking suspicion that the architect is more obsessed with innovative design than the comfort of the building's inhabitants. Frank Lloyd Wright provided a favorite role model for the profession: When one of his clients complained that a leak in the roof made dinner guests a little soggy in rainy weather, Wright suggested moving the dining room table.

A current trend, driven both by the architect's need to survive fiscally and the client's need to obtain service, has required all parties (architect, client, and constructor) to be more responsible in personal transactions. This somewhat coerced symbiosis has a positive spin: *Collaboration,* and likelihood of a satisfying project. Chicago architect Gigi McCabe-Miele believes that active participation and cooperation by the client are necessary prerequisites to every successful residential project: "So much depends on the owner, how much they understand the architect's role and how much they trust you."

Conflicts and Closets

"We can't keep our marriage together unless we have separate closets." After a brief assessment of the impact of her statement, Nancy managed a smile and a pat on the arm for her mate. Larry, unruffled by his wife's blunt comment, continued spooning his Shredded Wheat. I glanced at my associate who imperceptibly raised his eyebrows in confirming appreciation of the first clients of my new practice.

Several weeks earlier, the office of Andy Pressman, Architect received a telephone call from Nancy. With a smoothness and tone of authority rivaling that of an anchorwoman, she rapidly summarized her need for "professional services." Wanting very much to hear that Nancy had learned of my firm from the publicity surrounding a design competition win, I inquired about referral source. Matter of factly, I was informed that I was one of the "very few" firms listed with the local chapter of the American Institute of Architects that would take on projects budgeted below fifty thousand dollars in construction costs. "Reputation had little to do with my calling, if that's what you're asking."

Nancy (of Larry and Nancy) continued her telephone monologue with a description of "our global needs." I attempted to interject something about waiting until we could meet face-to-face, but Nancy insisted that it might be more "cost effective if you would begin prioritizing."

At this point, I felt compelled to learn a bit about my potential client, and since this was the Washington, DC area, I couldn't resist asking whether Nancy worked for the government. "Yes, I'm an analyst with a subcontractor in Pentagon City." Congratulating myself on such perceptiveness, I figured I had this one typed; whatever it was she wanted would be functional, perhaps minimalist, and modern in style (given the tight budget). Maybe there *wouldn't* be clippings from *Architectural Digest*.

Nancy began to elaborate: "My husband Larry—a lawyer—(for my nosey benefit) and I are planning a significant expansion of our home in Alexandria. We want kids and a new bedroom suite for us and you'll probably have to push-out one end of the house. Now, my cousin is at Princeton—her second year in the School of Architecture—and she has some wonderful ideas about style we want to incorporate. In fact, you may want to consult with her."

I mustered a rather anemic, "Uh huh." I wanted to know more about the exact location of the site and this seemed like the moment to broach the question. Not surprisingly Nancy had done her homework and was able to recite pertinent facts of the newly enacted regulations that specified constraints on building within the flood plain of the Potomac. Didactically and with perhaps too much speed, I ventured that "Unique constraints often inspire unique architectural solutions, so this is not necessarily a problem at all. As for style, well, the marriage of any notions about style with the facts of the site is what influences the expression of the addition—so, I'm not willing to discuss style by itself just yet."

Silence. Thinking I may have come across sounding too stiff and smug, I waited for Nancy to either hang-up or argue with me. Instead she countered with: "Just as long as we can use the antique railings from the old courthouse auction that. . . ." The sentence trailed off, allowing me to suggest that we might arrange a meeting at their house to talk with her and Larry personally and actually see the place.

The House

Our visit with Nancy and Larry had a pronounced domestic flavor. We arrived on a rainy Saturday morning and were greeted on the front walkway by two dogs. The scene was one we were later to recognize as prophetic. A sweet-tempered and slightly overweight retriever looked up with one of those sluggish dog smiles accompanied by a slow tail-wag. At the same time, with a loud and strident series of yelps, a tiny terrier flung itself from the shrubs into our path. Dancing over and in front of the sleepy retriever, the creature frustrated our forward progress. After what seemed like an eternity in the otherwise peaceful neighborhood, the side door opened and Larry stumbled out.

Rubbing sleep from his eyes, Larry nearly tripped over the untied lace of a moccasin slipped loosely on one of his large feet. He regained equilibrium and motioned for us to follow him into the kitchen. Before he was able to begin talking, a compact woman with aggressively frizzy hair bounded down the stairs and scolded the three of us. The gist of the outburst was our too early arrival and, "Oh, I'm Nancy." Following this energetic display we gathered around the kitchen table and the full story began to emerge. Between bites of multigrain and sesame cereal, Nancy explained that prior to consulting the American Institute of Architects for architectural firm listings, they had obtained proposals from at least two home builders. While apparently sound and slightly under their budget, the schemes appeared boxlike and altogether unrelated to the character of the house, its site, or the neighborhood. With a slightly effortful gesture of deference, Nancy seemed to be affirming my telephone talk. Larry remained half-asleep and apparently half-interested.

Looking at her huge sportwatch, Nancy announced she was late for the 10K Riverfront Shuffle. Moving out the door she directed her husband to "Show them the file."

The file was a vast collection of magazine and newspaper clippings and excerpts of letters from the talented cousin. The range of circumstances, styles, and budgets represented failed to make any sort of impression on the lethargic Larry. When we had finished leafing through Nancy's file, Larry quietly, slowly, and relentlessly maintained that he preferred a "legal motif," built around "found objects" rescued from old municipal buildings.

By lunchtime, Nancy had returned. We told ourselves that at least we knew the worst: We had elicited the entire inventory of Larry and Nancy's contradictory preferences. We had listened well and empathized with both clients without alienating either one. We had tried to bolster their individual and collective self-esteem by acknowledging their taste and their goals. We gave assurance that with just a bit of compromise, we were on the verge of putting together a comprehensive list of functional requirements. The aesthetic aspect would naturally flow from the architectural responses to these requirements. Larry and Nancy seemed appeased if not pleased by this summary.

Field Survey
The clients departed to various corners of the house, and my associate and I began the tedious survey of the existing condition. In the absence of original plans, any structure must be precisely measured and completely photographed. The resulting data are then translated into a set of plans, sections, and elevations from which the architect begins the new design. In the case of Larry and Nancy, we began with our documentation of the interior. I directed my associate to a long, narrow laundry room on one side of the house, while I unsheathed tape measure, kneepads, and camera in the living room at the other end. There is nothing like sketching and dimensioning a room from the

bottom-up to help one fully experience its contents and character: The layers of dust, petrified animal waste, occasional socks and underwear, bagel remnants (with and without evidence of cream cheese), and a curious assortment of ersatz American Indian artwork. There were prints, wall hangings, and carvings deposited behind and under furniture and appliances. A few of the pieces actually made it to a wall or shelf, though these were in the minority.

Working our way to the second floor was analogous to moving a rock and surprising two insects. Even the sedentary Larry seemed to dart toward the stairs as we approached the bedroom. Nancy was already moving downward in a blur of postrace Birkenstocks. In quiet resumption of our work upstairs, we felt something new. Trepidation, dislike, even revulsion gave way to an eerie sense and that we were privileged. Larry and Nancy had entrusted us with the intimate details of their daily lives. There is something sobering about rummaging in a stranger's bedroom. My associate and I cast silently admonishing glances at each other and conducted our work with the implicit understanding that we were, on some level, charged with a sacred trust. Larry and Nancy were really saying: "Here is our life, our confusion, our hopes—now help us to make it right." We pushed and sorted through the mess and filth with new resolve and affection for our clients.

Wrestling with Design and Presentation

My associate, who holds degrees in psychology, is first a clinician who knows how to spot depression—and rub it in. Over my shoulder I heard him say, "There are no bad clients, only bad architects. Someone famous said that. I think it's probably true."

"Look," I said, "This is an incredibly difficult project; I'm really agonizing about how to give these two what each of them seems to want and meet the objective requirements too."

Two weeks of intensive brainstorming, model building, and drawing followed. We far exceeded the scope of services outlined in the agreement signed early on by the clients. The project had to and did assume a transcendent importance. We were going to help these people in spite of themselves, and create a work of architecture.

The challenge was to modulate the scale of the relatively huge two and one-half story volume of the addition. The somewhat whimsical architectural response involved a high degree of articulation of the components of the design. This had to be accomplished while gracefully preserving and enhancing the modicum of charm and character of the original house. And so, it was with pride and great expectations that I telephoned Nancy and Larry to set a date for presentation of the preliminary design scheme.

Again it was a Saturday, and a rainy one at that. Protecting blueline prints and quarter-inch scale model with hastily assembled plastic bags from the local dry cleaner, I set off toward Alexandria and destiny.

In retrospect, I'm still convinced I made one of my clearest and most persuasive presentations. I am also as certain that Larry and Nancy were happy with what they saw and heard. I would even say they were delighted. Larry displayed some animation and Nancy was disarmingly sweet. With their check and their blessings to proceed with development of construction details, I sped back to the office in an exhilarated state.

On Thursday of the week after the presentation, I received a call from Larry and Nancy. Larry expressed their apologies, but after "sleeping on the design, there were some revisions." Nancy who had picked up an extension chimed in with a matter-of-fact recitation of all the changes she'd been thinking about "and really needed." But Larry appeared to be developing a backbone right then and there. He began to assert himself and then fight with his wife. He insisted on the priority of his own list of radical changes in the design. These seemed to align with Nancy's only in their departure from the substance and the very spirit of the design that they had so warmly embraced just four days earlier: "The valley in the new roof is likely to leak in five to ten years. It looks terrific but I don't want to spend money to maintain it."

My attempts to moderate were ignored as the dispute spiraled and escalated. I managed to end the event by affecting a slightly comic and somehow professorial voice and delivering a stern, "I think that's enough, people!" We scheduled a meeting at Larry and Nancy's that Sunday to reevaluate and clarify the situation.

Late Saturday afternoon, the office answering machine played the following message: "Hi Andy. This is Larry. Nancy and I see no need to meet tomorrow. We've decided to table all plans for new construction at this point. Thanks for your help. We'll give you a ring when we're ready to hook-up again. Bye." When you are a struggling and still idealistic architect fresh from two hours

FIGURE 1-1
"Before" rendering illustrates the awkward existing back elevation with mechanical equipment shed in the left foreground. Drawing by Andy Pressman.

of bad tennis and you get a message like this one, well, let's just say that some basic existential questions are raised.

What Should Have Been Different

The preceding story showcases a client who is tough—a product of a rushed and high-pressured life style, and a well-founded but sometimes hypervigilant consumerism. For my part, as a young architect, I was unprepared to assert myself effectively. The two parties in this case were mutually challenging and subtly antagonistic, and collaboration never really occurred.

The client arrived on the scene with a set of needs and preferences and with a propensity to place the architect in a subservient position. The interaction between client and architect became an uncomfortable skirmish for control of the way in which design issues were addressed. From the very outset, the architect's creative power was diluted and generally undermined. My response was ineffectual: First injured, then judgmental and punctuated with brief, albeit honest, attempts at educating, empathizing, and accommodating. Still striving to provide good quality design, I developed and presented a scheme that the client was never predisposed to seriously consider.

A responsible physician could no more be talked into sacrificing expertise simply to give a patient what he wanted any more than a lawyer would allow a client to formulate his own defense. The responsibility of patients and clients to participate

FIGURE 1-2
"After" rendering illustrates the proposed back elevation transformed into a new composition, maximizing three-dimensional potential. The addition contains living room and porch with master bedroom suite on the second floor. All new construction was required to be raised about a half-level above ground in response to flood plain regulations. Design and drawing by Andy Pressman.

FIGURE 1-3
Napkin sketch (left) attempts to capture the best features of the original house: Sharply angled gables, proportions, and dollhouse quality. Back elevation (middle) shows how the porch continuously wraps around the facade to unify disparate elements and provide a strong base for the new superstructure. Perspective view of the side yard (right) illustrates how the trellis is extended from the base of the porch and weaves up and down to announce the back entry. This side of the house was built up to the zoning setback line and therefore could not be manipulated in three dimensions. Drawings by Andy Pressman.

actively is certainly crucial to the success of treatment, litigation, or architectural design, but there is a distinct division of labor that must be preserved if meaningful collaboration and successful outcome are to occur.

The outcome of this particular case might have been different had I gently but directly defined my role along with its intrinsic and necessary authority. Perhaps this could have happened at the client's suggestion of consultation with an otherwise uninvolved family member who happened to be a design student. I might have said: "No, I will not likely consult with a student, but I will pay very close attention to your wants and needs and develop a comprehensive inventory of your requirements. It is then my job to generate a design response to this inventory and other factors. In addition to you and your husband, I may elect to arrange consultations with other engineering professionals with whom I have worked, and whom I know to be fully trained and experienced. So, bare with me—this is how we as architects have learned to provide you with the best possible professional service."

The statement above fundamentally changes the tone of the exchange between architect and client. Regardless of the outcome that ultimately remains in the hands of the client, the clarifying confrontation returns an appropriate measure of control to the architect. If the client accepts the conditions of the relationship, the architect is then free to perform the service for which he or she was trained.

A necessary qualification to all this assumes that the client has selected the architect on the basis of the quality (including aesthetic dimensions) of past work and references.

``All Great Architecture Leaks´´
(Quote by Frank Gehry)

Just in the way Theo Petrakis said the word "wood," you knew he was a craftsman. "Of course I can make you a lattice; I make so delicate it's a tracery!" He hugged me, shook his head with a smile, and glanced approvingly at his tattered copy of the plans. This last gesture was for the benefit of my clients, Mark and Vicki, and I was amused. The little man was not only a reliable contractor, he was a

salesman who understood that the enigmatic architect had to be af-
firmed by the person who was actually going to build the project.
This was especially true for Mark and Vicki.

The Project

Mark and Vicki came to me through the owner of a local business for whom I had done some space planning and renovation design work. Their children were preteenage, and they all lived in a large "traditional neo-Georgian style" home from which Mark also conducted his suburban orthodontic practice. The affluent neighborhood, on the north shore of Long Island, NY, was lovely with gracious houses and beautiful old trees that gave the surroundings a tranquility and elegance.

The design problem involved a boxy back room added many years ago that jutted awkwardly into the cleft between the two gently angled wings of the house. Apart from some nice brick-work, its single redeeming aspect was central location. Standing at the rearmost wall, one could look down a grand entry hall to the front doors some 35 feet away. Mark and Vicki hoped to "take full architectural advantage" of this regal entrance to an existing Kleenex box of a room. A glance at a lush garden beyond the box immediately stimulated my image of glass block and trellis as a way of opening up the house to the outside, and maintaining privacy. The clients further envisioned a den, a library, and a "cocktail cove," all communicating casually with the entry hall. It was one of those make it spectacular-but-modest, soaring-yet-intimate tasks that is such a genuinely intriguing as well as challenging problem for the architect.

Since Mark and Vicki were insistent that construction begin as soon as possible, I made their project a priority and within a week had preliminary concepts depicted in sketches: Three-dimensional renderings, plans, and cross-sections were mounted on large illustration board panels.

Trial by Jury

Filled with the excitement of an accelerated schedule and pending construction, I marched confidently into the initial presentation of my preliminary design. Not only were Mark, Vicki, the kids, and pets in attendance, but there was a stern jury of what appeared to be a room full of neighbors. Apparently I was designing not just for Mark and Vicki, but for their peers, whose approval seemed to matter more than a little. I began by de-

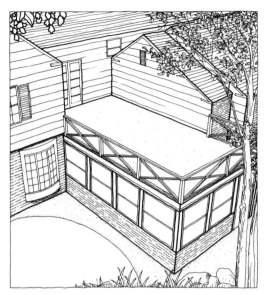

FIGURE 1-4

Perspective drawing of the existing condition: A backyard afterthought, an empty box interposed between the two wings of the house. A special directive by the clients was not to increase the volume or area for fear of rejection by the town's review board, and fear of a substantial increase in tax liability. Drawing by Andy Pressman.

FIGURE 1-5

The back room reinterpreted as an extension of the main entry axis, reinforced by a barrel-vaulted skylight and terminating in a glass block apse. Trellis framing wraps around the new structure, reconciling the awkward array of exterior surfaces and roof lines. Drawing by Andy Pressman.

scribing my idea for a barrel-vaulted skylight extending the grand hallway and terminating in a glass block apse. A delicate layer of trellis on the exterior would wrap the edges of the apse, and the adjacent walls would be shaped to gracefully unite the back room and the house. I continued with my presentation, indicating how the interior was laid out so that all the desired functions could be accommodated. Natural light would play a major role, taking full advantage of ever-changing shadow and leaf patterns from the heavily wooded yard.

I was quite startled by the response. Without so much as expressing an appreciation of the effort or at least acknowledging my first attempt at design, the interrogation began. A gentleman who looked like Jacques Cousteau observed, "With those angles and that long skylight, you're risking all kinds of water coming in, and as we all know, flat roofs eventually leak."

An obviously sophisticated woman asked, "Would you say more about the sources of historical allusion in your work?"

A younger, black-clad creature with a slash of dark red lipstick wondered, "Could you identify any opportunities for infusing your solution with deconstructivist themes?"

Then, a large man wearing a down vest asked the inevitable, "What about solar?" and, "I assume this is 'green' and 'sustainable' with no harm to the environment?"

Mark and Vicki presided in silence, apparently evaluating my every inflection during the onslaught of questions and comments, which had little or nothing to do with my design proposal. Every attempt I made to relate the discussion back to the work was lost in waves of tangential and exhibitionistic monologue. At least the gallery was successful at entertaining themselves for the afternoon.

My anticipation of referrals and a backlog of work from worshipful neighbors had all but vanished. Posturing like a harried politician at a press conference, I ignored a question and caught Mark's eye: "So, Mark, what do *you and Vicki* think about the scheme?"

The reply came almost instantly. "If your Mr. Petrakis can build it so it doesn't leak when it rains, then we love it!"

Somehow, I seemed to have cleared some rite of passage. The jury mingled, conversation reached a comfortable buzz, and a uniformed maid emerged from the kitchen to serve beverages and snacks. A little unsettled but happy with an approval to continue, I allowed myself to relax in this truly bizarre scene, and enjoy the prospect of the forthcoming construction.

Contractor as Ally

As I developed Mark and Vicki's design, I also cultivated my relationship with the contractor, Theo Petrakis. Though I suspected he really wanted to be Anthony Quinn, Petrakis obviously loved his work, and took pride in his talent and his network of subcontractors. He was also capable of improvising in the field. With old houses full of all manner of quirks just waiting to be uncovered, a builder like Petrakis could help to avoid extra costs to the clients. In light of the limited budget, however, it took a long lunch with promises of magazine coverage to get him to join the team. With all the drama and eye-twinkle of his Mediterranean soul, Theo Petrakis exclaimed, "Yes, I will do it—for you, my good friend!"

Not quite three weeks later, Petrakis dropped by the office at eight-thirty in the morning, proclaiming, "I smell coffee! And if I'm wrong, you better put some on!"

Petrakis was actually quite obnoxious, but it was impossible not to like him. Apart from coffee, Petrakis wanted to let me know that he had completed his bid and was on his way to

FIGURE 1-6

Floor plan of the remodeled space, with its discrete zones of seating and entertainment electronics. The forms and materials were inspired by a softly curving bay and built-in seating of the existing breakfast nook. Drawing by Andy Pressman.

BUILT-IN SEATING

ENTERTAINMENT CENTER CABINET

SKYLIGHT ABOVE

CENTER LINE OF ENTRY AXIS, APSE, AND SKYLIGHT

TRELLIS

GLASS BLOCK APSE

FIGURE 1-7
"Napkin" sketch at eye-level. The outermost layer of exterior skin (the trellis) is sloped to match the rhythm of nearby roofs, and arched above standard-size window and door units. This creates the illusion of arched glazing without the associated greater cost and detail. Drawing by Andy Pressman.

personally submit it to Vicki. Revealing a bit of appealing insecurity, he wondered how many other contractors were following through with bid proposals. I told him that Mark had asked that I send sets of construction documents to two other builders of his choice. As if to reassure himself and me, Petrakis raised his mug and made a toast: "To our victory, fame, and fortune, eh?"

With that, he set his mug down with a jarring crack, turned theatrically, and exited. I savored the moment, grinning and shaking my head. However, the mood was not to last.

The Resolution

Three days later, a letter arrived from Mark. It was typed on his professional letterhead and it stated that he and Vicki had decided not to execute the addition as designed. The reason for this decision was twofold: One involved his assessment that "There is a clear and present danger of the roof leaking." The second reason was the cost of construction that, while not exceeding their budget, "Was too out of line." Mark continued to explain: "I determined that the subcontractors were significantly inflating their bids. They would do so upon arriving at my house and taking note of our very high standard of living." This practice of alleged bid inflation was one that Mark insisted he "detected without fail." He concluded his letter by saying, "Our decision is a matter of principle as well as money." The notation at the bottom of the page indicated that a copy of the letter had been sent to Theo Petrakis as well as the other contractors who submitted bids.

What Went Wrong

It seemed as though another visit to Fred's Place, my hangout for regrouping and reevaluating, was in order. Indeed the soothing ambiance of the dining room (which always seemed to be in an off-hour mode) promoted satisfying reflection. I hypothesized that I had allowed Mark and Vicki to get hung-up on the construction details—such as the roof issue—and they then lost sight of the big picture, the design solution itself. By presenting the more conceptual aspects of the scheme, it was apparently assumed that I had little control over, or interest in, the more technical aspects. I may well have outsmarted myself. My associate, on the other hand, offered an alternative explanation, one that I found more appealing both intellectually and emotionally, but far less likely. He ventured the possibility that these successful "forty-something" adults might be having a lot of trouble with aging. The back room project was a concrete symbol of an approaching postparental stage feared by my clients. The room stood for a life-stage in which the couple's leisure would be spent entertaining, and—alone—with each other. I replied, "If you become any more superficially clever, they may accept you into that lovely jury of neighbors who attended my presentation."

At this point, I felt I had to do something different. The business of retreating to lick our wounds and rationalize was becoming unacceptable. I suggested that we "drop in" on Mark and Vicki, not to attempt a belated defense of our design, but to quietly find out what really happened. Ever since I launched my own practice, I had been solemnly admonished by my mentors to avoid work in the residential domain. Specific reasons were never forthcoming, only a kind of, "It's too terrible to tell," in combination with a not so vague smirk. I wanted to illuminate this corner of architectural lore, and I would start with Mark and Vicki.

My resolve to drop in translated to an unannounced visit about a month later. I was driven, perhaps by pure curiosity. So I found myself behind the wheel of my Honda pulling up to the curb in front of the familiar brick house. After no one answered my ringing and knocking at the front door, I proceeded toward the rear of the house, hoping I would find at least one family member there. I paused at the garage door which was half-open to accommodate several heavy corrugated cardboard boxes of immense proportions. On one side was stenciled, "Fox Valley Gazebo, Model Number 1509A."

I didn't need to go any further. Mark and Vicki had elected to forego the building process and to purchase a factory-made structure to be placed in the middle of their backyard. It struck me as quite clear that people who are spending their own money on the place where they live may be reluctant to embrace an architectural intervention, something so often perceived as abstract, expensive, and risky. Maybe there was a certain amount of validity in the mock psychological explanation of what had happened, but I now believe that there are some homeowners who are just not receptive to the process and product of architecture. My failure here may have been in not recognizing this, and encouraging Mark and Vicki toward a more distinctly architectural solution.

The Sauna and the New Jersey Turnpike

"One job superintendent heard he would be working on one of my jobs and he got scared. He started jogging for thirty minutes every day to train in case I attacked somebody. I'll quit architecture when I lose that emotion. You've got to really fight."
—Architect Tadao Ando in an interview with
Progressive Architecture, June 1993.

Meeting the Clients
The deer approached the baseline of the tennis court, pausing only to nibble on one of the potted geraniums that was in front of a small bench. From the breakfast alcove where I sat with Alex and Emily, it seemed incongruous that this scene was unfolding only an hour from New York City.

Alex was an international banker and his wife, Emily, was a mother of three who was also a part-time sculptor. Although located on five beautiful acres, their newly purchased house was too small for the growing family, and did not fully exploit the rural site. During the initial contact with Alex, I learned that the probable architectural scope of work would involve a renovation to the existing house as well as a significant addition. Upon my meeting with the couple, these expectations were confirmed. I was also struck with how delightful and sophisticated this family was, without any trace of affectation. Alex, Emily, and their children were nice people—*and* they had a subscription to *Architectural Record!*

As time passed and we grew closer, I liked them even more, and I discovered their one flaw. My associate called it "episodic technophilia." Every four or five days during the course of design development, I received a telephone call, usually from Alex, that would go something like this: "We just read about this new automated, voice-activated butler system that can execute hundreds of household tasks with voice command—and there's a modem or something that enables a link with the car phone; I could turn on the sauna or Jacuzzi from the New Jersey Turnpike on my way home from work."

I would patiently listen and respond by acknowledging the seductive luxury features now available with several home automation systems. The image of Woody Allen's movie *Sleeper* merged with my childhood memories of *The Jetsons*. It was hard not to laugh at the enjoyment and fascination with which Alex and Emily pursued microchip technology. And it was sometimes frustrating when this preoccupation excluded discussion about more significant and relevant design issues. But this was a trivial matter in an otherwise ideal architect–client relationship. The architect–contractor relationship, however, was another matter.

Meeting the Contractor

The only time I ever lost my temper occurred at the first meeting with Nick, of Superior Construction Industries. Nick was the general contractor whom Emily and Alex chose to coordinate all the construction work. (I continue to wonder about the nature of Superior's other "Industries.") Superior came highly recommended by neighbors who had been very pleased with a new garage Nick had built for them. I entered our meeting looking forward to establishing the kind of team ethic that would neutralize the historically adversarial architect–contractor relationship.

Nick and I sat facing each other at the small table in the breakfast nook. Emily and Alex were visible outside on the court, hitting a tennis ball back and forth. Nick began by pre-

FIGURE 1-8
A view of the new addition (on the right). It includes a guest suite with private entry above a two-car garage. Design by Andy Pressman. Photo © Norman McGrath.

senting me with a wrinkled and smudged business card depicting a disembodied roof on a background of light green. The telephone number had been crossed-out, with a new one penciled-in above. Already feeling a bit like the cliché elitist architect, I returned the favor with my immaculate white and gray minimalist card. Stuffing it in his breast pocket, he said, "Alright, let's do it."

The Conflict

Nick began to list design changes that he felt were required to meet the budget that he proposed, which had been agreed to by the clients. The result was a completely different project. At first it was his tone more than the substance of what was stated that got to me. Then the wave of anger hit as I became aware that under the guise of meeting the client's budget, Nick was attempting to cut his costs by bullying me into accepting changes that would motivate me—the quintessential sensitive guy—to dynamite the "tainted" project. When Nick went on to admit that Alex and Emily had not been appraised of his proposed new plans, I accused him of attempting to make unilateral decisions to increase his own margin of profit, to the detriment of design quality. Then the sparks began to fly.

FIGURE 1-9

(Right) A goal in designing the guest/garage addition was to relate it to the existing house yet distinguish the functions. Beams unite existing and new roofs and form an entry trellis. (Left) The lacy, two-story volume of the guest entry becomes a circulation focus. It contains stairs to the suite, and paths to the garage and adjacent existing studio. Photos © Norman McGrath.

Nick stood up, slammed his fist on the table, and screamed, "You obviously have no field experience! Your construction details are just pretty pictures; me and any other builder would go broke fast if we built that kinda crap. My advice to you is learn to work with real life, kid."

I stood up myself and shot back, "You are not the architect. Don't you dare dictate design to me or to my clients. If you promise to do a job for a certain budget, that's your problem! You can't alter the drawings to suit your own purposes after you've agreed to a price. Furthermore, if you had any difficulty or suggestions, why didn't you call me while you were developing your bid?"

Some movement outside drew my attention for a second and I caught an unintended glimpse of the tennis, and it made me hesitate. A couple of hundred hours of design work may have

FIRST FLOOR/Addition

Studio

Entry

Up

Two Car Garage

SECOND FLOOR/Addition

open

Dn

Guest Living Room

Roof below

Guest Bedroom

Balcony

FIGURE 1-10
Floor plans of the new addition. Design and drawings by Andy Pressman.

Existing

KEY PLAN

Addition

been saved in that instant. Catching my emotional and physical breath, I knew it was either make peace fast, or risk dragging Alex and Emily into the escalation.

I looked back at Nick, shifted gears, and as softly as I could, proposed a meeting of the minds: "Listen, I'm very good. I suspect you're very good. I know we can learn from each other on this project, and that may mean we can produce something special—which could ultimately reward us both far in excess of pleasing Alex and Emily."

Nick interrupted, a faint smile beginning to appear, "Not many of you guys defend their position that way, I respect that. I'll tell you what, let's go through my problems one by one and see if you can help me to bring this baby in with some sane numbers."

I quickly agreed, and in fact we were able to make revisions that did not profoundly alter the spirit of the design, and were more cost-effective. Of course, I shook for three days, but I learned something about the importance of old-fashioned politics in the service of getting the project built. Not that this was any simple or easy matter; Nick was an unwholesome character at best, and this was not going to change. However, he and his crew could be influenced and made more flexible in providing appropriate service.

Ruthless gestures on my part such as arriving during construction armed with fresh doughnuts, bagels, and Danish did much to break down antagonism and resistance. My associate's informal supportive visits with Nick and his lieutenants, usually around quitting time, allowed me to address problems the following morning (we played "good architect, bad architect").

I jokingly predicted a new building industry specialist—a "construction psychologist" who would interpret architect to contractor, and vice versa. I envisioned a *New Yorker* cartoon in which the properly bearded therapist sat between two portable couches with the framework of a partially completed structure in the background; on one couch an oversize bow tie would be visible, on the other a hard hat. "Why are you so angry?" the caption would read. The image was too close for comfort.

Construction

Emily, Alex, and their children remained in good spirits throughout the course of construction. In an undertaking of this scale, disruption of home life is more the rule than the exception. Certain phases of the work seem to produce more distress than others. One of the worst periods occurs when drywall is installed and finished. White dust is everywhere despite the ubiquitous plastic sheet barriers. Pets become walking time bombs ready to leave a white imprint on a suit or school clothes at the most inopportune moment. And there is always the mud that is tracked in by everyone entering the house. While all this falls into the category of temporary yuppie hardship, the discomfort and inconvenience are nevertheless sufficient to discourage many from embarking on a project.

Why is it that only *some* people are able to initiate and then follow through with large residential additions or renovations remains as a tough question. In the case of Alex and Emily, their confident vision of the future seemed to drive their motivation, and support their commitment. Equally important was their faith in both the architect and contractor. This promoted

FIGURE 1-11
(Top) The project also entailed raising a section of roof on the existing house for a new second floor master suite. Natural light from new skylights penetrates into the foyer below. Photo © Carl Weese. (Bottom) The new second floor plan of the existing house. Design and drawing by Andy Pressman.

NEW SECOND FLOOR/Existing

everyone's personal investment in the project, which naturally resulted in an extraordinary effort.

The New Yawkas

The political climate in the state of Maine can be characterized as one that insists upon restraint, tact, and a respect for tradition. Over the course of many pleasure- and business-related visits to the Pine Tree State, I have found the above characterization to be absolutely accurate, with a single exception in the person of Bob Down, of Down East Realtors. Bob contends that his people were "Maine-born as far back as the state and longer," but you get the feeling he has as much credibility as Mr. Haney on the old Green Acres television show.

I first met Bob on a classic motionless, subzero winter morning with the sun just coming up in a cobalt sky. I pulled into his parking lot between two mounds of crusty snow and came to a stop in front of the office door. Before I unbuckled my seat belt, a large, corduroy-wrapped man swung open the door and bellowed, "C'm on in out 'the chill!"

The Deal

Bob ushered me inside and introduced himself as a "simple man who raises sheep and picks a few blueberries, and a' course I do a few land deals as well." (I knew that he did a tremendous commercial real estate business.) Bob said that he had recently been lucky enough to seriously interest a couple from New York in buying a small vacation house. Bob continued: "They're nice folks, and they want to explore the possibility of making some architectural changes. They wanted to know if I personally knew of any architects, so I said, 'Ayuh.'" (He had a talent for affecting the Maine accent that out-of-state tourists have come to expect.)

Bob went on with his story. "So, I took the liberty of giving them your name. Now, if I'm able to show a prospective buyer an old fixer-upper, say, and in the same breath name a big city ah'chitect with local ties, well, my Gawd, that helps me make the sale and it keeps you in work. Sound good?"

The apparent package deal Bob was offering to the couple from New York seemed to involve a real and well-defined little project. Without much more detail, I agreed to take on the job. Yet again, I would learn that the absence of a direct relationship with the clients can be disastrous. I should have known as Bob exclaimed, "Well, that's great! Let me take you to breakfast to celebrate." Then, in a conspiratorial aside he said, "They'll go through money like green corn goes through the new maid!"

The interior of Bob's Saab had just gotten warm as we approached the promised celebratory feast at the Kracked Keel, between Arby's and a drive-in muffler repair garage. During the ten-minute drive from the office, I had learned that the New Yorkers were named Samantha and Murray and that they were both in film production, and were preoccupied with factory outlet shopping. Proximity to L. L. Bean was as important as views of the rolling fields opposite their proposed new home.

As Bob spoke, I felt increasingly comfortable about this particular project, since it was going to be "clean." That is, Bob was acting as my client, and I would supposedly deal only with him. The ideal immersion into the lives of the homeowners would be avoided, but in this case it might be alright—Samantha and Murray did not seem as if they would be a couple in search of architecture.

Bob inadvertently affirmed my initial impressions by talking further about the clients. He had gotten the message that "Las Vegas style" was a recurring theme in their lives. In the case of the house renovation, it translated to a bathroom "the size of Sebago Lake" with a two-person whirlpool set in a marble platform, towel warmers, his and her sinks, a shower with dual heads, a "steam environment," a make-up station, and a hidden, fold-down ironing board. This bathroom was to complement what amounted to a hotel suite that was to be designed within the shell of a farmhouse dating from 1800. Bob concluded with a chuckle and an afterthought, "I forgot to mention, the lady has—I ain't exaggeratin'—a roomful of clothes, and she wants 'em somewhere, somehow in the bedroom."

Returning to a more mainstream and business-like dialect, Bob opened a briefcase and removed a list of requirements for the renovation that Murray had assembled. The detailed list had been faxed to Bob's office from Murray's company, Glitz Productions. In addition to the bathroom/hotel suite Bob had described, Murray specified the need to convert an adjacent room to a "rustic and personalized stage set for entertainment."

Instead of a maid or butler, I could envision an assistant director commanding, "Action!" as a moose would run across the yard at regular intervals. While this was going on, Samantha and Murray would be reclining in their canvas chairs, sipping something blanc, and awaiting the arrival of guests from the coast.

The Drama

A few weeks after our breakfast at the Keel, I had an opportunity to meet Samantha and Murray. Bob persuaded me to present the design scheme myself; his not so subtle tactic was to claim that, "If I make the pitch, I might not be up to the sophistication expected by the New Yawkas, there's a chance it might not fly, and I might blow the whole deal." Bob's manipulation was transparent, but he had a point. It was not sophistication I was concerned about, it was "production values."

I arrived at the office of Down East Realtors ahead of time so that I could carefully set up my scale model and drawings. Bob sat at his flea market desk while I positioned myself on the painted picnic table he used as the "conference room."

The office door opened and a short, bald, heavy-set man entered, accompanied by a tall, dark-haired woman. Both were dressed in identical parkas that covered tan safari outfits. Their effusive greeting may have surpassed Bob's country welcome.

Following the introductions, Samantha and Murray sat at designated places in front of the picnic table, and I began my presentation.

"Nice prop," Murray interrupted, while grabbing the model, balancing it on his knee, and making it difficult for me to concentrate on the project description. Not even halfway through, Murray broke in again, "We like it—we're going out for a bite—where can you get a good lobster roll around here?"

Then, Samantha began to cry. With a thick forearm, Murray hooked his wife at the waist, swept her toward the door, and whispered to us, "We'll see you back here after lunch."

Murray returned to the office alone and fired me. He explained, "It's always very difficult to end a relationship—but we just feel that you were not able to capture Sam's imagination, and Bob, take no offense—maybe we should investigate other options."

FIGURE 1-12
Floor plan of a proposed new master suite including bedroom, bathroom, home office, and lounge. The requirement for space-efficient storage of the client's large wardrobe is met with a motorized clothes conveyor, similar to that used in the neighborhood dry cleaner. Drawing by Andy Pressman.

Battery Steele

A couple of months later, I received another call from Bob. He wanted a "private consultation, to bounce a few ideas about," for something like two or three hours. This consultation would occur without Samantha and Murray's knowledge, and was designed to help Bob prepare appropriately to ensure the feasibility of his latest state-of-the-art proposal—which involved the conversion of abandoned artillery batteries to luxury housing and studio space. The concept of our couple from New York holed-up in an old bunker was somehow right; I took the job.

I met Bob the following week on the ferry wharf at seven in the morning. Bob's idea was actually intriguing: The reuse of hardened coastal fortifications (which had been built for the defense of our key harbors during the early part of World War

FIGURE 1-13

(Left) "Before" sketch of the room adjacent to the existing bedroom, with a low ceiling of yellowing acoustical tile. (Right) "After" sketch showing newly exposed cathedral of roof pitches with new skylights. Drawings by Andy Pressman.

FIGURE 1-14

View to adjacent room from the bed. Glass block, located between studs in the load-bearing wall, allows natural light to penetrate into the bedroom and visually lengthen the suite. Drawing by Andy Pressman.

II) has generated sporadic enthusiasm and some creative efforts. The fortification we were to assess was located on an island only 15 minutes away via the city ferry.

We boarded the sturdy little vessel a little after 7:30. The red and white bows of "Abenaki" sliced through the chop and tossed salty spray to the deck. The surface of the harbor sparkled and the view of the islands was beautiful. The friendly beat of the big diesels below slowed to a steady thrum. The trip was over too quickly; we were approaching the dock at Casco Island. Fresh bread and boxes of groceries were off-loaded along with us, and a group of children rushed by in the opposite direction to board the ferry for the return trip and junior high school in the city.

Map in hand, we made our way to the island's perimeter road. Pretty houses with just-planted gardens dotted the sides of the road. A dog barked, a screen door whacked shut, insects buzzed, and birds sung. Patches of tall grass and tiny yellow and blue wildflowers completed a perfect New England spring day. The road veered left toward the ocean side of the island. Houses were sparse, and a chilly breeze called for windbreakers. The transition in scenery and climate grew increasingly dramatic. Trees and shrubs disappeared, replaced by marsh, rocky beach, and a sheer expanse of the sea.

I felt Bob grab my arm. He pointed inland. I looked and felt a shiver that had nothing to do with the chill. About 70 yards in from the road, embedded in a long bluff was a massive and eerie-looking concrete structure. Above a dark, cavernous opening was a thick, cantilevered cap shielding the now empty mounts for the long-gone artillery piece. This was Battery Steele (see Figure 1-15).

I took photographs and made quick sketches as we advanced through the scrub and marsh toward the huge bunker. Bob had briefed me about the installation on the basis of what he had heard through contacts on the city planning board. However, nothing prepared me for the impact of visiting the site. The contrast between the harbor and ocean sides of the island certainly was part of it; but the thing itself produced an unsettling and ominous, yet very magnetic feeling.

My consultation report included documentation of a 500-foot-long subterranean tunnel connecting Battery Steele with another emplacement less visible from the road. Storage vaults built on either side of the tunnel constituted a total of 20,000

FIGURE 1-15
Field sketches of the World War II bunker (right) and watch tower (left).
Drawings by Andy Pressman.

square feet of enclosed space. There was some vandalism and graffiti that I speculated might be attempts to humanize the place, but overall, it was in excellent condition. In view of this condition and proximity to utilities and the road, I emphatically recommended adaptive reuse. Even if it would assume the form of an avant-garde studio for Samantha and Murray, there seemed real potential for giving Battery Steele new life.

Successful professional politics can indeed make strange bedfellows. I believe that the overarching lesson here is *not* to rule out even the most obnoxious personalities as clients—they may lead one to the more interesting, important, and ultimately satisfying projects.

Archiphobia!

In the following essay, "Archiphobia!," Joseph R. Provey (based in Fairfield, CT) draws on his extensive experience as a journalist, editor, and observer in the world of home improvement. Provey sets the stage for an examination of the often highly political "impasse" be-tween architects and their homeowner clients.

Throughout my 15 years covering home improvement trends, I've always been fascinated that many homeowners opt for a cautious approach to architecture and design while others are willing to experiment. For the former group, it's okay for a family room to be a big box with windows, as long as it connects to the kitchen. Perhaps there is a half-round window or cathedral ceiling, but that's about as adventuresome as things get. And the budget isn't always the determining factor. Folks with big budgets are just as likely—or rather unlikely—to be experimental as people who remodel on a shoestring budget.

There *are,* of course, lots of reasons for being conservative about making unconventional changes to the space in which we live. For one thing, being different can get expensive. For an-other, untraditional designs haven't been subjected to the test of time, and they don't always work. Doing things differently can also mean a lot of your time, because client input and in-volvement are crucial. And, finally, if you let your idiosyncrasies show in a home, what will a prospective buyer say down the road?

It boils down to a general fear or reticence about hiring any sort of design professional. And even if a homeowner works up the courage to engage a professional designer, the results are often unsatisfying. It's almost as if most of us don't believe in the need for designers—and those who do are unsure of how to successfully tap the designer's creative energies. The fault isn't ours, alone. Designers can be exceedingly poor marketers of their services and, in some cases, unwittingly breed distrust.

The bottom line is that a professional designer can make a difference—if you pick the right one and take the time to learn how to work with him.

Why Homeowners Don't Hire Architects
Acquaintances like to tell me about their personal building and remodeling projects. At a recent neighborhood pot-luck, for ex-ample, Bill and Elise shared tales about the construction of their summer getaway on the Rhode Island shore. Among the first questions I asked was whether they had used an architect to help them with the project. The answer was, "No. We did the design ourselves." That's the answer I usually get—one that

never ceases to surprise me since just about every home improvement magazine or book recommends hiring a design professional.

The homeowners I talk to have lots of reasons for avoiding designers of all stripes, particularly architects. They range from, "My builder can do what I need," and, "They cost too much," to "My wife's a graphic designer and can do it herself." After years of hearing comments like these, I decided to put the question to several architects across the country whose work I admire and whom I knew would be candid with me.

What follows is a list of the basic reasons homeowners give for steering clear of architects, the architects' reactions and their advice for getting around the impasses.

IMPASSE 1: *You have to be rich.*

Budget is the biggest reason many homeowners avoid architects. But the problem is not necessarily what that architect charges in fees, note several architects. In fact, it often has more to do with the costs homeowners think will be tacked on to their projects as a result of added complexity or expanded scale.

Duo Dickinson, a Connecticut architect (and *Fountainheadache* contributor—see "Measure Twice, Cut Once" in Chapter 9) suggests there are two brands of political style among architects: Those who subordinate the client and those who subordinate themselves. Architects, he explains, are traditionally recognized for the product—not the process—of their design, even though the success of the latter is essential to satisfy most clients.

New York architect Ernie Harris puts it this way: "Will the architect build a monument to himself?" Fears like this, he says, are potent, since homeowners don't have much experience with architects—"and they've all read *The Fountainhead.*" He adds that not many people understand how architects work or what they do.

Dickinson comments that architectural schools often imbue students with the idea that design is a magical process that develops more from inspiration than from client need. The houses that are held up as great examples of architecture usually are discussed and studied without much said about the role owners played or should have played.

Dickinson maintains that many architects haven't come to grips with the dilemma of simultaneously serving both the homeowner and the taste "gods" of architecture. It's not uncommon, he says, for a young architect to win a job by appearing sensitive to what the clients want, figuring (consciously or not) he can win them over to his concepts later on.

IMPASSE 2: I won't be able to resell my house if I accept an unusual design.

It's difficult enough to let yourself be a little different. It's even tougher if you think you'll pay an economic penalty for it. Harris says there's some justification to this, but what you can get away with depends on where *you live.*

California architect Heidi Richardson runs into the resale concern often and believes that most residential architects are sensitive to it. She also feels that the fears may be overblown. "After all," she points out, "if you like it, there's bound to be someone else who will, too." Richardson also observes that second-home buyers tend to be less concerned with rules like "it must have three bedrooms and two baths." They tend to be more willing to think of their own needs and desires first.

IMPASSE 3: Your builder objects.

It stands to reason that builders are politically uncomfortable with architects. For centuries, after all, builders performed the design role, themselves. They *made decisions based on local styles, regional materials, and traditional building techniques. Architects tend to be viewed as extraneous, even after nearly 130 years of trying to forge relationships with homeowners and builders.*

Many builders think straightforward jobs don't require an architect—and if you're sure that's what you want, they're right. But keep in mind that builders have an agenda of their own, too. They want to build your house, addition, or dormer as efficiently and with as few surprises as possible. Their profit depends on it. If an architect creates something a little unconventional, the proposition becomes a bit riskier for the builder. Several architects noted that it helps in these cases to find an architect who understands the building process or, as one architect puts it, "knows his way around a two-by-four."

Just as important as finding an architect fluent with residential construction is finding the right builder, notes Harris. Heidi Richardson guides her clients toward builders who have executed demanding designs in the past. She also points out that this type of builder is very likely to appreciate architects. "The architect, while generally thought of as an agent of the homeowner, also can act as a buffer between the builder and an unreasonable or unknowledgeable client," she says. "In fact, some builders won't work without an architect."

IMPASSE 4: *Bad communication.*

Most architects don't help matters. They haven't marketed themselves to residential clients very well. Consequently, most people think of them as being exclusively for the wealthy. However, many architects who are perfectly qualified to do small-scale residential work don't want to. Narrow profit margins and a huge time and energy commitment are often cited as reasons to avoid the domestic scene.

The Right Reasons for Choosing an Architect

So, what can we say in general about finding ways around the typical impasses between architect and client? My advice to prospective clients is, don't fall for the wrong architect! Dickinson says you'll be far better off if you "search for someone who will do a 'we,' not a 'me' building—where the 'we' includes the builder;" in other words, find someone who is politically secure and unselfish. The trick is to make sure that whomever you choose to work with believes meeting clients' needs is the top priority. "Image mustn't terrorize need," says Dickinson, adding, "the *design process* should bridge the void between what the architect knows and what the client knows about himself."

CHAPTER 2

PRIVATE BATTLES IN THE PUBLIC DOMAIN

John Dixon, an editor at *Progressive Architecture,* has almost lyrically stated how architects can sometimes manage the myriad forces tugging at monumental projects: "The strength of architects lies in our ability to synthesize the sometimes contradictory impulses of today's society into responsive spaces and forms."

The following three stories embody the potential that Dixon has expressed. They concern highly visible and important projects *"with design at stake!"* The architects, Charles Gwathmey, Stanley Allan, and George Hartman, persevere against difficult odds to achieve design excellence for their clients and ostensibly for wider society. Scrutiny of their designs by special interest groups and the architects' formulation of a response (without diluting the original intent) are major components of creating great architecture in this realm.

Fusion of Old and New at the Guggenheim

Preservation and renovation involving all building types are issues that are becoming increasingly important as we approach the next century. Renovation of older buildings is rapidly accounting for the largest percentage of all dollars spent on construction. Moreover, the trend to recycle buildings and preserve those of historic import is consistent with the sustainability message from conservation groups.

The meaning and application of this effort are nowhere better crystallized and exemplified than by the addition, renovation, and restoration effort at the Solomon R. Guggenheim Museum in New York City, by the architectural firm of Gwathmey Siegel & Associates. Altering the Frank Lloyd Wright masterpiece was a provocative act, and the Guggenheim story yields much insight into the definition and practice of architectural design in this specialized world, as well as insight into relationships among architect, client, government agencies, and public groups.

Charles Gwathmey, one of the partners-in-charge of the Guggenheim project, is among a small number of world-class talents producing some of the highest quality architecture today. His firm has received over sixty design awards, including honors from *Progressive Architecture, Architectural Record,* and the National AIA. But, more important, he is a decent, forthright, and sensitive guy—the ideal combination of traits for one who must negotiate with distinctive clients and stakeholders—all of whom have their own special interests and agendas.

Gwathmey's point of view may contribute significantly to his effectiveness in reconciling the conflicts between those who often seem to lie on opposing ends of the "change" *vs.* "no change" spectrum. He is disarmingly eloquent about balancing a respectful appreciation of an original building while working to promote adjustments that ensure its continuing relevance and accessibility for a constantly evolving society. The project consists of a new 10-story annex (a limestone-clad rectangular tower)—which adds exhibit space and visually serves as a neutral backdrop to the existing building—and restoration and renovation of the Wright building.

What Gwathmey has to say about the unfolding of the Guggenheim project applies to "everyday" architectural projects in general. That Mr. Gwathmey and his associates were able to persevere and achieve a most successful outcome is acknowledgment that the application of the time-honored principles of history, logic, and creativity truly do result in design excellence.

My conversation with Mr. Gwathmey that follows illustrates the role and influence of the various players in shaping and executing this formidable project.

A Unique Commission

AP: I think it would be fascinating to hear how you successfully completed a project laden with so much controversy and emotion. It seems like an unbelievable achievement to gain approval from all the principal parties. How did you do it?

CG: You should know that the clients were always supportive. The interesting battle at the Guggenheim involved the preservation and historicist lobby—which in a sense became the counterclient. This situation may be more difficult than a challenging client—especially when they're explicitly the opposition. And I think it's a valuable lesson, not so much because of our perseverance, but because of the strategies we employed—the use of factual research and organized presentation that in a sense balanced and refuted the often emotional and irrational presentations that our counterclients continued to introduce. The six years of hearings and going all the way to the New York Court of Appeals became a lesson in controlling your temper and doing your research and presenting it in a way that was both emphatic and passionate as well as accurate.

AP: Along those lines, how were you able to maintain your cool and resolve in the face of such relentless and vocal criticism?

CG: I admit that when things were the lowest, I would always rationalize by saying, "Well at least what we were giving back to architects was hopefully documentation of legitimate preservation and extension." A lot of architecture, as we both know, is not realized but is part of the legacy of publication—and the hope always was that it would have some future research value and maybe some future realization. As an academic, I am interested in the *idea* of something as well as the *fact* of something—that's what carries you in these kinds of things.

AP: How were you most persuasive?

CG: We had constant hearings and many interviews with the press, who were predisposed, by the way, to favor the opposition. I think the most crucial series of events was that in the initial presentation, Edgar Kaufmann, Jr., who was regarded by the Board of Appeals (the hearing body in New York City—initially the zoning body), as **the** consummate expert on Wright—because of Fallingwater and because of his scholarship on Wright, testified against our initial scheme. He was very effective and was humble in his presentation style and knowledgeable as well—whether you agreed or not—it didn't matter.

When we revised the first scheme, I presented it to Edgar Kaufmann personally before any hearing. He reversed himself and wrote an eloquent letter—because he was sick by then—to the Board saying how responsive and sensitive we were to the initial criticism and that the second scheme, which was the one that was ultimately realized, was both sympathetic to and responsible to Wright's original vision, and in fact enhanced the building. This letter, in conjunction with the fact that Donald Trump was Kaufmann's successor as the expert on Guggenheim Museum additions, turned out to be a terrific advantage for us.

FIGURE 2-1

The first scheme: Model photograph of the proposed addition to the Guggenheim by Gwathmey Siegel & Associates that included space for art storage and conservation as well as increased exhibition area. Photo courtesy of Gwathmey Siegel & Associates.

AP: You turned Edgar Kaufmann into your biggest and most important ally.

CG: It would have to have taken some overwhelmingly compelling argument to dissuade him. In other words, he was the prime-mover in the initial ruling to have us revise our scheme. If he comes out for the second scheme and is still regarded as the expert, that is, changed his mind and supported the other scheme—the opposition would require some much stronger argument. They did get William Wesley Peters who designed the Annex to testify, and he both misrepresented his original Annex and he was undoubtedly ailing, perhaps senile. I was polite in reminding him both of his writings and quotations about his addition, all of which contradicted what he said to the Board.

AP: So it's at that point where you felt the public audience was on your side for the revised scheme?

CG: I think the public audience—the public legal audience— became swayed. We still had to go through that horrendous time-consuming process: After we got approval from the Board of Appeals, we then had to get approval from the New York City Council, which was a very emotional presentation because they ring the bell after two minutes, and you're supposed to stop talking, and I refused to stop talking. I said, "I've been testifying for four years, I've worked on this project for eight years, and no bell is going to stop what I have to say."

AP: How did they respond?

CG: They let me finish. And it was very convincing. I said, "The opposition has misrepresented, exaggerated, distorted, and it has actually, in fact, presented false conclusions throughout this process. We're at a time now where we have to reevaluate the word and the idea of preservation: What does it mean?" This whole presentation through the legal approval process was six or seven years.

AP: And the criticism was so frankly nasty.

CG: Oh, it was unbelievable. I was vilified. You know, I mean, I'm sort of a sensitive guy—believe it or not—sitting there and listening to people say these things about you—it's not easy when you know that you're honest and you know that you have history on your side.

AP: How did you handle the personal attacks during this process?

CG: You get a little bit thick-skinned; you also wait for the moment—as would a competitive athlete—you wait for the moment to find the weakness. So you have to be patient. And when you see an opening, you have to go in for the score. There's no question, it felt much like that.

AP: What part does charm play or is it more how you educate people?

CG: I don't think it was my charm. I think that everyone realized that we had a very compelling argument: Frank Lloyd Wright *proposed* an addition and Taliesin West *built* an addition. There was history and precedent on our side that everyone was trying to ignore.

AP: Were you very disappointed about the rejection of the first scheme?

CG: Yes, I was. I was disappointed because I believed in the energy of it and the fact that it was much more counter-pointal as a consummate collage. It would have been controversial and dynamic but still in the spirit of the original building.

AP: But your arguments didn't seem to be quite as compelling or accepted for this first scheme in terms of convincing Edgar Kaufmann.

CG: Two things happened. One was that Michael Graves had simultaneously presented the first scheme for the Whitney and the whole issue was so hot—respecting existing buildings and status quo, and the preservationists were really out there beating the bushes. Paul Goldberger didn't help. The arguments were so irrational.

AP: Do you think you could have gotten the first scheme approved at a later point in time?

CG: I don't think we would have gotten *any* first scheme approved. I think the strategy that we finally understood in hindsight was that no matter what we would have presented first would have met with opposition.

AP: What would you do differently now? Would you have developed a totally outrageous first scheme?

CG: A lot of people thought our first scheme was outrageous. I don't think you can go back. I think the lesson lies in the proof of respectfulness, and understanding the ways in which we reconstituted the original building: The new work has enriched it, it has expanded it, and it still hasn't in any way detracted from it; and it's made it a living extension rather than a static, dying building representing an institution. I think the true test is when architects see it, and architects are not that generous to other architects, as you know, and they are unanimous. I mean that there's a sense about this that's so irrefutable in a way.

AP: That must be very gratifying.

CG: Yes, that's it. I think that, in the end, is where it's at.

AP: What about the strategy: You mentioned that no first scheme would have been approved.

CG: That's in hindsight. I think if we came back now and wanted to make an addition to our building and propose the bay window again, I think it would cause a huge reaction, but I think there would be a lot more sympathy toward it, given the proof of the reality. But I don't think that's going to happen—which is too bad.

AP: How did you adjust or develop your communications—both verbal and visual—to the different groups who were in positions to judge the design?

CG: What we realized was that each time the opposition was able to raise a question of doubt in the view of any board, that we had to answer it. So we were always aware of, because of the process, positions that in general were going to be taken. We would establish our presentations to subtly address them (before they were stated by the opposition)—because the appliee goes first and the opposition goes second, and then we have a right to answer.

AP: So you tried to anticipate the specific problem issues?

CG: Yes, there was a certain amount of anticipation and definitely a certain amount of innuendo that we would cast before the opposition—which would tend to diffuse many of their arguments as they were being stated. It was done extremely unemotionally and factually, and we had terrific visual tools. We did terrific drawings, and we had documentation.

AP: It's interesting that with this very logical and informed presentation approach, you ran up against a stone wall with the first scheme. It still strikes me as a bit curious given the way in which you were so successful in getting the second one through.

CG: Well it's amazing to me that the different perception of the schemes was so violent and so vast. I don't think there's such a big difference, personally. But I think the preconception of what was respectful as opposed to what was counterpointal was a huge issue. The word "competitive" was used. The perception that our building was *competitive* with the original or *detracting* from it was driven by very emotional responses that were not about the history of intervention and collage, but were simply very conservative and subjective reactions.

AP: Did you have a difficult time at that point when the first scheme was rejected—going back and redesigning—was that a difficult step for you?

CG: That's a good question because I think typically one would, but at that point in time the new director came on board, whose vision of the museum was very different from our original client. He changed the program, which allowed the Frank Lloyd Wright building to be all exhibition related. We shouldn't try to keep our storage on the site, and we shouldn't try to keep conservation, we should make this building the exhibition center and we should go off-site—freed the program—and allowed us to reevaluate the program in a sense to make an uncompromised gallery flow.

AP: So you were essentially given a different project for the second scheme.

CG: Exactly. Which was a very fortuitous occurrence. In this case with the existing specifics and the constraints, we ended-up with a more straightforward plan. It is about spatial integration of old and new. The organization responds to the ramp cycles and the interactions between the two buildings, with the idea of moving into the original, then out of it, then back in it again. The most controversial issue, however, may have been the *image* of the addition as perceived from the west—from Fifth Avenue. The building that had become a cultural icon in New York City still is recognizable as such even though the museum has increased exhibition space and offices by over 65,000 square feet.

Our original scheme, despite the fact that it included art storage and conservation, was still more or less about this spatial integration of the new and the old, as well as the renovation of the old. So it got clarified in the revision, and it certainly got refined because you continue working on something.

AP: But the major departure was the imagery.

CG: The major departure was façadal—which is a drag, actually.

AP: Is there anything more you would like to say about this project?

CG: I think the client deserves special mention. The Board of Trustees and the president of the Board of the Guggenheim and the Director were, despite immense pressure, absolutely committed to the realization of the project as an institution.

FIGURE 2-2
View of the expanded and renovated Guggenheim Museum from the northwest. Photo © Jeff Goldberg/Esto, courtesy of Gwathmey Siegel & Associates.

And they never second-guessed us—which is part of the answer to, "What allowed us to carry-on?" We didn't have the battle of the client saying, "We can't go through this anymore—let's retrench, let's reevaluate our whole philosophy." We were bucking the landmark date—that's what the opposition was really trying to do—to delay the process until the building turned thirty (in 1989) and could achieve landmark status [therefore postponing or preventing new construction].

AP: Your client, even though changed, was totally supportive all the way through.

CG: Yes. It had a lot to do with selecting the next director—I wasn't at the interviews but I knew his position coming in was in support of the addition. The other thing I think is true is that if you have an academic basis or a theoretical basis that can be both documented and supported by history and by factual interpretation as opposed to purely subjective, emotional references, then you are going to prevail. I don't think there's any question about that. It's whether you can stand it—that's all. The lesson in the end is that preservation is interpretive and that it doesn't mean simply restoring the status quo. It means there is a possibility for enrichment through interpretation that is both a tribute to the parent building and visionary as well. Visionary in the sense that a new person is coming to an existing condition and seeing something beyond it—which is possible.

AP: Was the change in program driven by, to a large extent, the negative reaction?

CG: No. The vision (which was supported by us 100 percent) was that if we could take the large rotunda and make it a referential space that was in the tradition of a courtyard or cloister, reinterpreted, without requiring it to accommodate *every* temporary exhibition, we would free something that had never been possible before. We weren't obligated to use the large rotunda only for temporary exhibition; it was an available space that could be intervened into creatively. And we had all this other new support gallery space that fed and referenced to it, allowing it to have the ability to, in a sense, free-float. So the whole dynamics of making the Wright building totally public and accessible and about exhibition, and 90 percent of the addition about exhibition—which is what brings the public to the building—I think this was a terrific reevaluation in strategy. This also helped us, by the way, in our later presentations, because what we were offering to the public was a view of Wright that had never been seen before. So culturally, intellectually, preservationally, archeologically—it all supports in my mind the idea of inventive preservation that extends, enriches, counterpoints, and allows you to see something both in the frame of history and in the frame of a new set of perceptual dynamics—which I think is great.

AP: I continue to be struck by how supportive the client was throughout this process.

CG: I think if they weren't, we never could have kept going. Because the cost, and the delay, and the threat of coming to the Landmarks Preservation Commission and not being able to do anything were so pressing, to give up the opportunity to get something right was, I'm sure, on their minds.

AP: Were you the only architect considered initially in the selection process?

CG: We were retained to make a study of the existing conditions and to evaluate the institution's goals. We learned the collection, thought about the aspirations of what could be, and also defined a maintenance/renovation program for the existing building, which, by the way, was in horrible shape. I mean it wasn't even insulated—did you know that? It was a Gunite shell. The air conditioning hadn't really worked for

FIGURE 2-3
New seventh-level ramp and upgraded skylight dome. Photo © Jeff Goldberg/Esto, courtesy of Gwathmey Siegel & Associates.

10 years, there was no humidity control, and all the glass was single glazed—no ultraviolet filters. So over the years, systematically they just kept closing the building down.

AP: Your existing condition analysis led to further exploration?

CG: Yes, I think an architect had to make a proposal for alternate possibilities. I think they felt very comfortable with us; they felt we were sympathetic to both the institution and to the building. The two year "getting to know one another" and also having a reasonable reputation, just continued. I don't think there was any question about stopping and interviewing other architects after that happened. I don't want to use the word lucky, but it was a way of backing into a major commission.

AP: You put yourself in an indispensable position.

CG: Unique!

For the Glory of Washington[1]

Stanley Allan, Chairman of Harry Weese Associates (HWA), Architects and Planners based in Chicago, was the project manager for the Washington Metropolitan Area Transit Authority stations (which serve the District of Columbia as well as suburban Maryland and Virginia). HWA was responsible for establishing the architectural concept for all stations and structures, and coordinating the architectural design work with the engineering design team.

Metro received a National AIA Honor Award for architectural design in 1983. The jury for the award stated: "The manner in which many professional disciplines and regional interests were brought together makes it one of the most successful public transportation projects of recent times." And Wolf Von Eckardt, then architecture critic for The Washington Post, *wrote the following on November 20, 1971:*

> *[Metro] brings with it a quality of design that is rare in municipal architecture and unheard of in American public transportation since the great railroad stations at the turn of the century…suddenly there is noble spaciousness—a Roman vault with coffered ceilings, as in the dome of the Pantheon….This time we really have something. This*

---

1. © 1994 Stanley N. Allan. This excerpt taken from *For the Glory of Washington* is under copyright by Stanley N. Allan, FAIA.

time the national capital region is setting new standards of excellence for the country and possibly the world to follow.

Occurring in 1966 and 1967 in Washington, this excerpt succinctly tells the story of Harry Weese Associates (the General Architectural Consultant), De Leuw Cather (the General Engineering Consultant), the Commission of Fine Arts, and Washington Metropolitan Area Transit Authority (WMATA)—protagonists with design at stake!

Separate and Equal

Our Washington Metro client's approach to the design for the rapid transit system led to a decision to select separate engineering and architectural consultants, acting as coequals, each reporting directly to the National Capital Transportation Agency (NCTA), yet coordinating their work together. This decision grew as a result of many discussions in Washington during 1954 and 1955 among Darwin Stoltzenbach, John Rannells, Paul Thiry, Nat Owings, Henry Dreyfuss, Fritz Gutheim, Karol Yasko, Charles Horsky, William Walton, and many others.

This was an unprecedented breakthrough. Generally, all previous American public works projects were designed by the engineering professionals with very little if any conscious architectural design input. When Walter McCarter succeeded Darwin Stoltzenbach as the NCTA administrator, he endorsed this idea wholeheartedly. In a collateral action, the Office of Architecture was set on a par with the Office of Engineering.

General Architectural Consultant

Piloted by Chief Architect John Rannells, the NCTA took this approach in their search for an architect, keeping in mind San Francisco's recent architectural setback in the design of their stations for the BART system. Architect Don Emmons had been selected to provide an overall sense of design unity for all of the BART stations. Unfortunately, he was placed under contract to the joint venture of engineers. After a long period of internecine strife, he felt constrained to resign in the face of the engineers' determined opposition to his efforts to give BART stations a cohesive architectural character.

To avoid another architect–engineer standoff, Washington's architect was therefore to be directly under contract to the NCTA, independent of the engineers. It was clear that only by maintaining a certain level of independence could the the architectural contribution lead to a higher state-of-the-art. John

FIGURE 2-4
*Plaster model of the
protostation vault built for
the fourth presentation to
the Commission of Fine
Arts in October 1967.
Photo by Stanley N.
Allan.*

Rannells clearly understood the nature of his mission: To significantly improve the image of transit facilities, relate this system in its setting in our nation's capital, and produce an exemplary system attractive to Washingtonians and visitors—both national and international.

One of our biggest challenges was how to impart our ideas constructively to the General Engineering Consultant (GEC). They had no way of knowing the extent of what an architectural concept meant. Was it to be merely decorative, devoid of structural implications, especially for underground stations where there was no exterior design requirement, or were the architects going to become involved in the structural design, too? At this point the GEC waited to see what we would produce and waited for us to show the extent of our architectural intentions.

We didn't know until years later, as confided by De Leuw's president, Jim Caywood, that there was, embedded in their contract, a requirement to pursue the design of the stations. And as Jim stated to me, they meant to do just that. So, unknown to us, we both had adversarial roles. This fact underlines the dominant regard held by the engineering profession for the scope of their domain on large public works projects. Perhaps one of the GEC's strongest advantages was their assignment to perform all cost estimating for their work as well as ours. In retrospect, I don't think the GEC knew just what to do but wait for us to show our hand. They respected our firm's reputation and by common knowledge knew that Harry Weese was a talented and successful designer, well known in Washington by the cognoscenti, and quite likely prove to be a formidable protagonist.

The big issue the GAC faced, vis-à-vis the GEC, was that both were instructed to develop designs for column-free station trainrooms. It was a contest between our vault versus their box.

Thus, the battle was joined between the two consultants, each pursuing the same goal but with different frames of reference and different educational and professional backgrounds. The engineer's experience since World War II mainly centered on designs for the Federal Highway Administration's vast national Interstate Highway Program, not to mention design of dams, bridges, and tunnels. Their transit background derived from extensive railroad design, construction, and operation experience, as well as work for the Chicago Transit Authority and the Toronto Transit Commission. They had little or no experience working with architects who, in this instance, had a clear mandate to establish the ultimate station designs. De Leuw Cather principals—Jim Caywood, Ken Knight, Bob O'Neill, Al Bumanis, and their staff of 200 engineers—struggled through this difficult design process with us driven by their ingrained instincts as they saw their responsibility to create an economically feasible solution.

Amidst all of this design activity, our client commissioned Ammann & Whitney, under the leadership of their president, Ed Cohen, to make a comparative cost analysis of the GEC column-free box structure versus the gravity arch station cross section. Simply stated, their engineering analysis concluded that when there was an overburden load in excess of 14 feet, the arch was the most economical solution. Since all of the 45 below grade stations with the exception of two had an overburden load in excess of 14 feet, the selection of the arched configuration was further supported by another substantial advantage.

As it turned out, our mandate was taken up by the Commission of Fine Arts (CFA). Working for a client heavily influenced by the advice of their General Engineering Consultant, we did not underestimate the need to gain approval of our design solution from the CFA.

So, it became a joint CFA/Weese objective to balance the forces at work and prevail. The CFA members instinctively realized this unique opportunity must not be lost: To select a design concept appropriate for the formal dignified setting in our nation's capital. Ultimately, this off-setting search of a suitable urban design approach was to eclipse the otherwise rational engineering proposals. The engineers had not been invited to these meetings. CFA members, significantly, were interested in talking only to the architect.

Third Presentation

Our presentation to the CFA on Tuesday, September 19th, received the third rejection by its members. The meeting lasted more than two hours, during which the CFA members expressed themselves fully, articulating individual reactions to our presentation. At mid-point, Gordon Bunshaft compulsively seized one of our presentation boards and rapidly drew a sketch on its back. The sketch, showing a rough cross section through a protostation trainroom, replaced the stream of words or rather gave them a form—an idea he had for some time. At the second presentation, in June, Gordon made an offhand comment that, "The stations should be shaped like the inside of a thermos bottle, one station after another."

This sketch was not lost on Harry Weese's quick intellect, connecting it with our earlier vaulted station design. He realized the situation was not so far from correction as one might think. It was time to recognize that we now had acquired an additional client—one who would not be rebuffed—whose ideas in effect

FIGURE 2-5
L'Enfant Plaza station of the Washington Metro. WMATA photo by Phil Portlock.

would eclipse the approach dictated largely by engineering and budgetary considerations. This meeting proved to be the turning point in the balance of power over the nature of the solution. The commission members really interceded to become a design partner with Harry Weese through the sheer power of persuasion.

Jackson Graham's Memorandum

These experiences created an atmosphere that helped shape the client's General Manager's [Jackson Graham's] next strategic move. His gift for simplicity and seeing through complex situations was here to give him the ultimate opportunity to make an agreeable recommendation to his Board. He wanted no such controversy in the press such as BART had, nor one in front of the American Institute of Architects, much less a confrontation with the CFA. Armed with the imprimatur of the CFA, he was now able to go to his Board backed by the CFA as well as WMATA's own architect, Harry Weese, to substantiate his recommendation.

On October 30th, eleven days after the CFA approval, Graham submitted a memorandum to the Board on the subject of the subway station concept design. The memorandum is reprinted below; it is self-explanatory and presents a brilliant case for acceptance.

The First Final Design Contracts

At the executive session of the November 3rd meeting of the WMATA Board of Directors, Jackson Graham reviewed the status of the final design contracts to produce the bid documents for the first three stations, Judiciary Square, Gallery Place, and Dupont Circle. The first two had been contracted to Ammann & Whitney, with Kent Cooper as the associated architect, and the third to Kaiser Engineers. These contracts had been put on hold pending the outcome of the decision on the architectural concept. After a discussion of the situation, the Board unanimously authorized the General Manager to give these firms a notice to proceed, utilizing the general plan drawings prepared by Harry Weese & Associates and De Leuw Cather on the basis of the design concept for the vaulted station trainrooms.

WASHINGTON METROPOLITAN AREA TRANSIT AUTHORITY

1634 Eye Street, N.W.
Washington, D. C. 20006

October 30, 1967

MEMORANDUM FOR: Chairman and Board of Directors

SUBJECT: Subway Station Design Concept

  1. Attached hereto is a copy of the transcript of the October meeting of the Commission of Fine Arts at which the design concept of the subway stations was discussed. It is a particularly informative transcript of an important meeting, because there are clear statements (1) of the Commission's unanimous and strong support of an overall design concept, (2) of their response to the specific reservation felt by the Directors as to the desirability of the design concept and (3) of their serious view of their responsibility to the public in the opinions they state.

  2. The transcript also gives an insight into the friendly respect felt toward Harry Weese by Commission members who are themselves internationally eminent at the top of their various professions. Through their attitude toward our consultant, these people have come to feel themselves consultants to the Authority, rather than critics or watchdogs, and as such are able to give guidance that would be the envy of anybody able to assemble, and pay for, such talent. Parenthetically, the American Institute of Architects is even now scrapping expensive and thoughtful plans for their national head-quarters because of the influence of this Commission. The A.I.A., as owner of a national landmark in Washington and as the official body of American architects upholding aesthetics all around the country, found their carefully thought-out design unacceptable. As can be seen in reading the attached accounts, their President and top people were not able to move the Commission from its position, even after a joint meeting, and even such an "in-group" as this one is now revising its plan.

  3. Significantly, however, our position is even less tenable than that of the A.I.A. should we attempt, not to assert the worth of one plan over the denial of the Commission, but to deny the worth of another plan in the face of the Commission's unanimous and laudatory approval. To deny being bad is no shame, but to deny being good is a dangerous race to run because to win is to lose after already having been awarded the medal. We can not defeat nor afford to try to defeat the Commission on its own aesthetic grounds.

4. San Francisco's troubles have been mentioned often as
something to be avoided at all cost, and while they are now mostly
financial, there have been expressions by their own Directors that
began, at least partly, as aesthetic ones. Their public furor over
aesthetics was instigated by a consultant and siezed on by an eager
press as a hook on which to hang suspicions, doubts, and innuendo
about any person or aspect connected with the system. The idea of
this Board turning away a conscientious, gifted, and famous designer
who had the enthusiastic endorsement of the most prestigious group
of consultants anywhere would surely open the flood gates to public
doubts of the system and its direction, and create not just a bigger
flap than San Francisco's, but could jeopardize our very existence
in much the same way. And the course is a predictable one: a public
question of aesthetics raises doubts of the Authority's concern for
the public, doubts of their other consultants' work, and especially
doubts of the validity of cost estimates. The system becomes a
faceless bad guy and is fair game for anyone with a beef or a desire
to gain public sympathy for a cause. The public controversy that
ensues is not unnoticed by political and financial interests not
necessarily directly involved but who nonetheless have an influence
on the program. Finally, as the battle rages, the very voices of
reason and calm that are needed are not available, through reluctance
to join in what is by then a public brawl.

5. As with any question of taste or philosophy or human
qualities there can be no right or wrong answer, only opinions,
however formed. Just as there can't be a correct answer, nor proof
ever demonstrated, the advantage lies with choosing the course that
will support a change in direction later on. That course is to adopt
the system concept that has been recommended; it need be followed
only so long as it produces results that are acceptable. Whenever
the consensus is that it produces a dull or drab product, that design
can be rejected and the concept abandoned. The reverse is not true,
however, because once abandoned the system concept cannot be
recovered.

6. I can only recommend as strongly as possible that the
course of temporal acceptance of the single design concept be
followed, in the knowledge that it will not create a disastrous
controversy, it will allow design and construction to proceed on
schedule, it will allow economical design and construction costs,
and it is a course that, unlike its alternative, can be altered
should it be found unsatisfactory. This problem has now been under
discussion for six weeks, and its immediate clearance is vital to
continued progress.

Jackson Graham

Encls
as

Penn Plaza and the Design Review Board

Hartman–Cox Architects of Washington, DC won the prestigious American Institute of Architects firm award in 1988. In over 25 years of practice, they have consistently created buildings that are highly responsive both to surrounding context and to "multiple clients," as George Hartman, FAIA, would say. They are professionals who explicitly strive to provide genuine service to their clients, and aspire to contribute to the larger built environment — with all that the phrase implies.

The story of the design of a mixed-use project for a developer-client and the issue of responding to the criticism of design review boards, written by Mr. Hartman, is an extension of his architecture — concise, to-the-point, and appropriate.

Penn Plaza

Sometimes, you have to put a lot of faith in your architect. In 1987, a major downtown developer was pulling out all the stops to get approval for a new mixed-use complex just off Pennsylvania Avenue. The block on which the project was located contained a number of historic buildings of various heights and materials, and Hartman–Cox had devoted much effort to design what was hopefully an appropriate building for the site, with a modest tower to complement the Victorian turrets on the block.

The day of the crucial design review came, and we were scheduled to present late in the afternoon. Unfortunately, that day the review board was subjected to a plethora of towers; every new project seemed to include some overwrought projection. The board's mood was sour when the Hartman–Cox project came before them, and the verdict was disheartening: "The tower doesn't look right; take it off."

The developer was not happy. The logical response was to remove the tower and re-present the project. Upon reflection, though, this seemed the wrong decision. Maybe the review board was reacting less to what we did than to how we did it. We redesigned the tower, increasing its height by a full story and giving it better proportions. Understandably, the developer was anxious; they wanted an approval, not a tower, but they trusted us.

At the next review board meeting, we presented the new, taller tower. A nervous silence followed. Then a few nods were seen on the board members' faces. "We like it. The tower looks right. You fixed the problem."

In essence, it proved wise to listen closely to the review board, to read between the lines, and to respond to their concerns rather than their specific suggestions. They identified the problem correctly; we fixed it.

Politics, Feelings, and Details

I wanted to know more about George Hartman's reactions to the review board's criticism, his feelings about redesign, and his relationship to the client. I arranged for an interview.

Hartman responded in predictable fashion: "Don't add too much extraneous junk to this simple little article!"

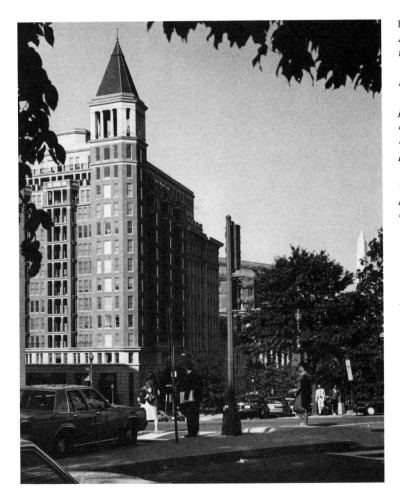

FIGURE 2-6
A view of Penn Plaza, the mixed-use complex by the Washington, DC firm, Hartman–Cox Architects. The redesigned tower, a point of contention with a local review board, relates to the tower on the nearby post office and the Washington monument, reinforces a pivotal corner point in the L'Enfant plan, and also recalls the towers traditionally associated with Washington apartment buildings. Photo by Alex Washburn, AIA, courtesy of Hartman–Cox Architects.

Hartman's elaboration portrays and further clarifies artful politics in support of design excellence, insight, and experience.

We recognize the existence of multiple clients. The client is *not* the owner of the land, *not* the design review boards, *not* the lender, *not* the tenant, *not* the person in the street, *not* the architectural press—*the client is all of them.* We are comfortable with the notion that just because somebody's hired us and is paying for our services, they are not the client; they're simply part of the client. You have to be a politician to make this point to the person who writes the checks. It's probably no accident that we're practicing in Washington. One needs to deal with a very broad constituency, and we try to show concern and respect for this larger constituency. Urbanism, that is, the preservation and enhancement of the built environment, is one of those things that we feel we need to practice. We don't always succeed in getting this message across to our clients, but we often succeed.

Relative to Penn Plaza: The tower modification *was not* a compromise (although I don't think there's anything inherently wrong with compromise). There were two components to the review board's criticism. One was identification of a problem and the other involved some specific suggestions to address the problem.

The Pennsylvania Avenue Development Corporation Board was *right* about the tower and *wrong* about what they told me to do. It's very easy to see the problem when you've spent some time on these boards—how you solve the problem is another story—there are many ways to skin a cat. We did not compromise the idea of the tower; we fine-tuned it without changing the fundamental character of the original concept.

There's no sense taking the tower off for one agency and having another agency that's already approved it say, "Where the hell is the damn tower? It had a tower when I approved it!" Then you get caught in a battle between two agencies, and anybody can look at the design and see that it's worse as changed. That's an indefensible position.

What's interesting and unique about this is that when you have really good people on review boards such as George White, Carter Brown, or David Childs—when you get three opinions of thoughtful, gifted, talented, perceptive, and highly experienced reviewers, you begin to understand that the stuff that they see wrong is indeed a problem. Now, what to do about it? I can't solve anything instantaneously in my own work, so it's unreasonable to expect that anybody else on a review board can do it. So you take the concern and deal with it, not the specific suggestion. *I've never seen a project that didn't benefit from further study.*

I remember one time, before I was a member of the Commission of Fine Arts, I was bringing in a project for Harvard University—Dumbarton Oaks—here in Washington. As we were presenting (the client was there, of course), I was showing two slide carousels, almost like an art history lesson, so everyone could see what this was about. Carter Brown said, "Left screen: Back-up three, please." I knew right then I was in trouble. I backed it up and Carter said, "Have you noticed how the existing building intersects previous additions? Why doesn't your work relate in the same way?"

I paused for a minute and looked at it and said, "There's no sense in your watching me think—I didn't see that, and if it's all the same to you, I'll see you next month." When I came back a month later, Carter said, "That looks much better now, are you comfortable with this?"

I said, "Absolutely, I just didn't see it." The client was horrified, but it went right through, bingo—this time. And it *was* better.

When you have a consensus of the review board, then you almost always know you have a problem to deal with. You can sometimes have a member say something and someone else will disagree—you don't have to deal with it. On the other hand, note who is making the comment and if it is justified—you might end up with a better building.

The important thing about our relationship with clients is that I spend as much of my time on *education* as I do on anything else—on my education and the education of our employees, consultants, clients, and public. When I talk about design, I'm talking about the relationship of buildings to their surroundings, to their users, to other buildings, and, of course, by extension, of buildings to their parts and parts to the buildings. Education is a wonderful thing because it's irreversible.

How do you effectively educate? *You spend a lot of time with people and you look at a lot of buildings with them.* Sometimes when we attempt to educate clients, and have explained an issue several times, they say, "Hartman, that's bullshit!" Maybe it is. And we have to rethink it.

Our clients tend to be supportive but also demanding and exacting. They will certainly come to us and say, "Okay, the job is high, I told you it was supposed to be thirty-five million dollars and it's thirty-seven—we've got to get two million dollars out of it. Fix it." Then there's the famous Mike Prentice line, "Hartman, how good is this estimate?"

"It's a good estimate—it's really close."

"How close?"

"I'm sure it's within ten percent—I promise you it is."

"Hartman, do you know what ten percent of fifty million dollars is?"

The estimate then got a lot closer. We have good developer clients and, by and large, they're repeat clients: Prentice Properties, Trammel Crow, Prudential, and Boston Properties. They hire us for appropriate jobs. One of the things that smart clients do is match-up the architects with the jobs. One of the things that smart architects do is match-up the developers to the job. We don't take every job that is offered even in these terrible times. We try to do work that is consistent with our practice and interest. We also don't work for clients who don't know what they're doing. We want a client that will pay a fair fee, has a fair budget, and a realistic time schedule. Most successful, smart people are educable; however, not all of their employees are, I've found out.

The lesson of this article is a very useful one. It's important to separate *what* is being done from *how* it is being done [Lou Kahn]. Remember Kahn saying he'd rather be doing the right thing badly then the wrong thing well. Of course, what you've got to do is the right thing well.

CHAPTER 3

COLLABORATION VERSUS COMPROMISE

Architects and clients working together—collaborating—to create a great design is clearly a superior alternative to sacrificing part of what each party wants or believes. There is a fine line between diluting powerful ideas—compromising—and developing beautiful designs to be most responsive to particular circumstances, requirements, and preferences. The skillful architect can educate clients about possibilities perhaps never imagined and can develop what Bill Lam calls (in his interview in this chapter) a "shared vision of project objectives," all toward making architecture. Helmut Jahn, FAIA, of the Chicago firm of Murphy/Jahn, concludes that, "Our best work comes from clients who know and support us because *our goals match.*"

Walter Gropius, the quintessential collaborator—at least among colleagues—had a policy in his office (The Architects Collaborative or TAC) for resolving the problem of too many or conflicting ideas in the design process. Sarah Harkness has quoted Gropius as proclaiming that to "Safeguard design coherence and impact, the right of making final decisions must be left exclusively to the one member who happens to be responsible for a specific job, even though his decision should run counter to the opinion of other members."

Charles Moore (whose inspiring story of designing a church together with its congregation appears next) has a slightly different take on the collaboration/compromise issue. Invoking *Goldilocks and the Three Bears,* Moore has said that "The extremes (too hot/too cold, too big/too small, or too hard/too soft) can be troublesome and uncomfortable but the balanced middle ground can be a pleasing compromise [that] is for me as admirable and truthful and meaningful and pertinent as any philosophy."

Collaboration at St. Matthew's

The late Charles Moore, FAIA, was perhaps the most brilliant **and** *service-minded architect of our time. The fact that his accomplishment must be explicated in this way is a sad commentary on the public perception of what an architect is supposed to do. This image has, in no small measure, been perpetuated by the portrait of the malignantly narcissistic Howard Roark character in* The Fountainhead. *That the architect is used as vehicle for Ayn Rand's views and is so misrepresented in such a popular book (an estimated 100,000 copies are sold annually) has, in part, resulted in an enduring focus on some of the negative aspects of the profession. (Revisit the often-quoted Roark statement: "I don't intend to build in order to have clients. I intend to have clients in order to build.")*

Architects who conduct themselves like Charles Moore, the antithesis of Roark, are not few and far between. His story of active client involvement in shaping the design of a church is a wonderful model: It demonstrates that beautiful architecture does not have to be created in a vacuum, does not have to be a unilateral vision of a single individual, and does, in fact, require heroism—to innovate, to compromise in some ideal sense, to learn, and to develop a meaningful, interactive relationship with the client.

Talented and secure architects are not only willing to accept clients at face value, but are also interested in eliciting input from representatives of all building users. Incorporating ongoing dialogue with the client into the design process and translating these data into an appropriate physical response are the only way a building can ultimately be considered beautiful.

Written just before he died in December 1993 (at age 68), below is Mr. Moore's fascinating account of a project executed with his Santa Monica-based firm, Moore Ruble Yudell, Architects & Planners. (He was an AIA Gold Medalist and former dean of the School of Architecture at Yale and chair at Berkeley, won numerous competitions and design awards, and was the author of several books including Water and Architecture, *published in 1994.)*

Around 1982, Buzz Yudell, John Ruble, and I were approached by an Episcopal congregation to design a new church in Pacific Palisades, a wealthy western suburb of Los Angeles near Malibu. Their original church had burned down in a forest fire, so they were in need of a new one. Since the parish had just emerged from a long, drawn-out conflict over the selection of a new rector (after its rector of some 30 years retired) they perceived themselves as not being able to agree about what day it was.

When the congregation started planning for the new church, they decided to include in the architect's contract a clause that any design would have to get a two-thirds vote of approval before construction could begin. We, Moore Ruble Yudell, were somehow hired with a general warning that no one would ever get a 67 percent agreement out of that parish on any subject, especially a design. We could imagine that, and thought that the only building the group would ever agree upon would be one that they had designed themselves with our professional help. The possibility of developing our own brainchild and then peddling it to them was out of the question, even if we had wanted to do that (which we didn't).

Facing such a task, we called on the services of Jim Burns, who had pioneered participatory design in his years with Lawrence Halprin. He helped us to organize and plan open design charrettes scheduled into four Sundays, each about a month apart. The first was spent in what Californians call an "awareness walk," looking over the site and filling notebooks with observations and possibilities for the site of their new church. Then we came back to lunch in the garden of the parish house and people worked on big scrolls of butcher paper putting down their dreams and strictures about the place they wanted. Then we went into the temporary church and brought out the materials of design and model construction: Fruit Loops, cellophane, school scissors, paper, and parsley. (Parsley is great for models because it wilts quickly so nobody can get infatuated for long with what has been produced.) Fruit Loops represented people, so that bits of the cereal could be easily lined-up, moved around, and arranged in various seating configurations. Each person or group made a model of how the church should be, with many serious discussions about how things should relate to each other. By the end of that session, people had made quite beautiful churches.

An important discovery we made early was that when we really pushed something, we lost it. It worked best to let the parishioners generate the ideas, and then to coax them into architectural expression. We sought to translate their ideas, including the contradictions, directly into design, while giving the church a clear sense of being connected to the site and to California's arts and crafts tradition. One contradiction that we had to somehow accommodate was the longing for seating in the half-round, but under a classic Latin cross plan with a nave and transept. They wanted to get as close to the altar as possible, but they didn't want to go so far around it that they were looking at each other. Another hurdle involved finding consensus between high church parishioners and low church parishioners. One high church lady thought that lofty ceilings were mired in sin and offensive to God, while many low church members vociferously wanted high acoustical ceilings to accommodate strains from the organ.

The magic moment occurred at the end of the second workshop when the participants all had the same plan. By the end of the workshop, we had a working plan that pleased everyone.

Next, we thought it might be interesting to make a kind of Rorschach test of slides, all mixed-up, with two questions to be responded to for each of the 80 slides. (1) "Do you like this?" And (2) "Would you like this for St. Matthew's?" It turned out that although they had all kept saying that they wanted a dark wood church (the former church had been that), the three slides of Alvar Aalto's white church in Vuoksenniska [Imatra, Finland] were the leading vote getters. The church that received the fewest and most negative votes—emphatically, "We do not want this for St. Matthew's"—was St. Peter's Basilica in Rome. Too Catholic, too expensive. So we at least knew something about what they did not want.

The third workshop involved our coming together with a set of building shapes in model form that would cover the plan shapes that they had come up with. The parishioners were asked to consider those and make whatever contribution of plan and enclosure that appealed to them. They came with drawings and were not afraid to give us rather strong orders: "More glass to the ground!" (The rector was opposed to this one since he didn't want his sermons to be in competition with the squirrels outside, but the feeling was very strong and he did some compromising.) But again there was almost complete agreement on what they wanted it to look like as well as what they wanted, and how they wanted it to function in plan. So we drew the results of their desires with a half-elliptical seating arrangement under a Latin cross roof with a bell wall, which has since turned into a tower, with lots of glass to the ground and a very simple interior.

FIGURE 3-1
*Charles Moore
(foreground) and members
of the congregation during
one of the participatory
workshops for the design of
St. Matthew's Parish
Church in Pacific
Palisades, CA. Photo
courtesy of Moore Ruble
Yudell, Architects &
Planners.*

We presented the drawings, made a model, and left it all for a month for the parishioners to ponder. After proposing some slight changes, they put it to vote, and we got an 87 percent positive response where we had needed 67 percent and there was enough invested enthusiasm to propel the money raising even a little past its goals so that there were funds, for instance, for the bell tower.

St. Matthew's is at once a simple chapel and a church with a rose window in it. It gives out double signals. On the outside, the broad, hipped roof is low at the edges, rising to a cruciform in the center, and cut away to create little courtyards and patios. Inside, the liturgical celebrations are framed by "triumphal arches" that carry visible steel trusses, with the arc of the pews mimicked above by arcs of lighting. The surfaces are made with Douglas fir battens applied to heavy plaster walls, so they are rich both visually and acoustically. With the considerable help of Tina Beebe, we made color, both painted and natural, an integral part of the church. Our goal was to balance equal amounts of artificial and natural colors—painted steel and plaster along with the Douglas fir, clay tile, and granite. Color also helped clarify the building—green and cool on the outside, rose and warm on the inside. We also managed to squeeze some art into the budget, so that a tree of life, a lectern, and a crucifix add layers of Christian symbolism.

The church was built and even won an AIA award. I'm often asked if we didn't feel a diminution of our creative satisfactions in sharing all these design decisions, and I have to admit that part of the province left to us involved putting a Latin cross roof over a half-elliptical floor plan, which seemed like something Alberti would have responded to enthusiastically. For me personally, the chance to be involved at St. Matthew's is evidence of the value in making a great paradigm shift from Yang to Yin or at least fanning a little bit of the wings of change. Being a part of making that church was an opportunity to work toward an architecture filled with the energies not only of architects but of inhabitants as well, and helping people to find something to which they can belong.

FIGURE 3-2
Axonometric drawing illustrates that there is indeed a cruciform, though masked by other forms branching-out at the ground level in addition to a number of hipped roofs. This responds to the parishioners' wish for semicircular seating within a more traditional sanctuary. Drawing courtesy of Moore Ruble Yudell, Architects & Planners.

WEST ELEVATION

0 5 10 20

SOUTHWEST ELEVATION

0 5 10 20

EAST ELEVATION

0 5 10 20

FIGURE 3-3

Elevation views reveal a more domestic scale at the perimeter, ensuring a good fit in the surrounding residential neighborhood. The contrast to the grand scale of the sanctuary is at once intimate and awe-inspiring. Drawings courtesy of Moore Ruble Yudell, Architects & Planners.

The Closest Kind of Collaboration

When an architect's client happens to be his wife, the Fountainhead-Ache could turn into a raging migraine. But when James Stageberg, FAIA, a Minneapolis architect, designed a writer's retreat for his wife, Susan Allen Toth, all they found they really needed to work well together was trust, flexibility, and an occasional aspirin. Asked to comment on their collaboration, they decided to report on it directly, with equal time, in the following dialogue.

James Stageberg, principal with The Stageberg Partners in Minneapolis, MN, is also a professor of architecture at the University of Minnesota. He and his wife, Susan Allen Toth, wrote A House of One's Own: An Architect's Guide to Designing the House of Your Dreams *(Clarkson Potter, 1991). He is now working on a memoir about his life as an architect, tentatively called* Architect: A Life on the Straight Edge.

Susan Allen Toth's latest book, My Love Affair with England: A Traveler's Memoir *(Ballantine, 1992), was published in paperback in 1994. She is now preparing a collection of travel essays about England, many of which first appeared in the* New York Times *travel section, to which she is a regular contributor. Her other memoirs include* Blooming, Ivy Days, *and* How to Prepare for Your High-School Reunion.

SUSAN: When James promised to build us a weekend retreat, a place where I could hide out and write, he asked what kind of house I'd always wanted. "An English country cottage," I told him without hesitation.

JAMES: Of course I had no intention of designing something with a thatched roof and leaded windows. I'm a modernist architect, always hoping for an ideal design of simplicity, clarity, and functional elegance. But I knew what she meant. She wanted something cozy, yet distinctive. "Cozy" is a word that has become unfortunately rather unfashionable among contemporary architects. I think it means a house that is welcoming, modestly sized, warm—a shelter, not a show-off. To create that kind of cottage, without being cute about it, or phony and quaint, was a real challenge.

SUSAN: I mentioned color too. English cottages themselves aren't usually brightly painted, but they're surrounded by wonderful gardens, jumbled-up blues, greens, yellows, pinks, and reds. Winter in the Upper Midwest has its own palette of color—grays, black, white—but that isn't enough to sustain me for months on end. I wanted color with a capital C!

JAMES: I also had to take into account our stunning site, a wooded Wisconsin bluff about 400 feet above Lake Pepin, a widening of the Mississippi River. So I tried out many versions of a design for Wind Whistle (the name borrowed from an English pub, because of the terrific winds that often blow over the bluff). Some of these were pretty awful, some not too bad. I illustrate these try-outs in the book Susan and I wrote about Wind Whistle and house design in general, *A House of One's Own* (Clarkson Potter, 1991).

SUSAN: I deliberately didn't look at any of these early versions. I didn't try to advise James on a design in any detailed way, because I just can't visualize an architect's plans in three dimensions. I had a hard enough time with plane geometry. And I trusted his skills. I'd already lived for several years with him in a house he'd designed. It was the first modern house I'd ever really liked. Most of them made me feel very cold; I can't stand a lot of chrome, icy surfaces, too much glass, no clutter. And I knew he understood how I felt about light, for instance, which I love. I did say things like, "You know I like to lie in bed and look out of a window into the trees."

JAMES: The final design has a dramatic cat-slide roof in front, swooping down over the guest bedroom. The whole roof is covered in cedar shingles that have been left to weather— about as close as I could get in a Midwestern climate to the feeling of thatch. The entrance side looks out over woods and a patch of meadow, which Susan promptly began to convert to garden areas. Our own bedroom, on the river side, has two sheltered walls, but on two sides it overlooks the cliffside trees. Susan can also look up through a skylight into the top branches.

SUSAN: When I saw that swooping roof, it did make me think of an English cottage—as though a little house were tucked beneath. Inside, the spaces felt right too, not so big I'd feel lost in them, and well separated. I hate rooms that all run into each other. I want walls, doors, lots of privacy. We once toured an architect's house that had a master bathroom with side-by-side toilets. No, thanks.

JAMES: I did get some grief from Susan about her study.

SUSAN: I told James my ideal was a room of my own upstairs where I could pull up a ladder after me. Well, I didn't really expect a ladder—how would I carry a computer up and down?—but that was my vision. So he did give me a room on the second floor all by myself—it's really the only room at the top of a winding stair—but then he couldn't resist adding a small sauna for himself just above, next to a crow's nest on the roof. And I turned out to have a ladder, but it is a ladder that starts in my study and goes up to the sauna!

JAMES: Since we almost never have guests at Wind Whistle, and I'm the only one who uses the sauna, there wasn't much traffic in and out of Susan's study. But she grumped about it.

SUSAN: I also hadn't expected the number of architectural friends, potential clients, past clients, and so on who asked James to give them a tour of the house. Every architect's wife (or husband) will know what I mean. A painter has a gallery where people can look at his or her work; an architect has a house, and people have to walk through it.

JAMES: So two years ago, when we were in England, visiting Monk's House, where Virginia Woolf had once lived and worked, we saw her small studio at the back of the garden. I knew immediately that was what I had to do for Susan. When we got home, I tramped around our five-acre lot until I found a place on the wooded bluff where I could just fit a one-room studio.

SUSAN: I call it my retreat from our retreat. This time I really did get my ladder, in the form of a short bridge. It isn't a drawbridge, but it gives the same effect. *Nobody* walks across without permission.

JAMES: When we built Wind Whistle, we also had some vigorous discussion about colors.

SUSAN: It wasn't so much discussion as a confrontation between two very opinionated people. James had always preferred natural woods, and he was known for his imaginative use of different shadings and grains and so on. But I wanted color, outside as well as inside. I remember when the house was finally finished, ready for painting, and James and Larry, our builder/carpenter, stood outside with me, pointing out how beautiful the cedar shingles were in their natural state. Larry said, "How could you *possibly* want to put paint on that wood?" But when you live with an architect, after a while, you learn not to be easily intimidated. I pointed out that I *was* the client.

JAMES: I knew better than to push too hard. So we picked the colors together, and I hoped for the best. But the day we drove down from Minneapolis, after the exterior had been painted—lemon yellow, with apple-green trim, and accents in a sort of pinkish red and mauve—I was plenty nervous. When

FIGURE 3-4
Collage of plans, cross sections, and perspective view of *Wind Whistle. Drawing by James Stageberg, FAIA.*

we walked out of the woods and stood in front of the house, I really blinked hard.

SUSAN: I loved it.

JAMES: Actually, before long, I did too. Susan trusted me about the design, and I (mostly) trusted her sense of color. We were so relieved that we both liked the exterior that we decided to experiment with color on the interior as well. I decided to have the ceilings given an unusual treatment. They are all wood, #2 knotty pine boards. Grant, our painter, applied a colored stain, then rubbed it off, leaving a color that still revealed the graining in the wood. In the living room, the largest space, the soaring ceiling is a soft blue, like the sky. In the hall, the ceiling is green, in another room, pinkish red. I had Grant prepare different samples so Susan and I could pick the right tone. We wanted what she called "garden colors."

SUSAN: We had some discussion about wallpaper, too. Modern architects I knew never used wallpaper. It was practically a dirty word. But I wanted some floral designs on a few of the walls.

JAMES: And she got them. I told Susan that of course we'd have to agree on something special enough to justify my covering up those handsome walls. We eventually found some marvelous Swedish hand-screened wall coverings, with very clear and bright colors, one with tulips, another with peonies. I felt fine about using them—sparingly.

SUSAN: That's really how we worked most of the time. I knew James would never agree to anything that damaged his design, and he knew the general effect I was looking for. We both ended up delighted with the results.

JAMES: In fact, the only real problem with Wind Whistle is that Susan now wants to be there all the time. My office is in Minneapolis, and so we do a lot of driving back and forth.

SUSAN: I think it is a great advantage to be married to one's architect. In our case, James knew me so well he could anticipate my needs almost without my asking for them. When I did really want something, I could fight for it straight out, without feeling timid or worrying I'd be upsetting him. James can be tough-minded, but he's no Howard Roark. I read *The Fountainhead* when I was nineteen, and I thought Roark was thrilling. But he'd be hell as a husband. And actually, when

I think about it, he'd be hell as an architect, too. Can you imagine what Roark would have said if I'd asked *him* for an English country cottage?

Contemporary-Traditional in Florida

Anchorman: *How does it feel to lose everything? You have no house, you have no transportation, you don't know if your children are alive—how does that feel?*
Hurricane victim: *Oh, God.*
Anchorman: *There you have it. Reporting live from the field, only miles away from my own winter home, I'm Jim James.*

It was a near perfect commission; a call from a local celebrity; a request for help in designing a second home/dream mansion in Florida, and a budget to match the scale of the project. I say "near perfect" because the constraints were significant and would have an impact on how much freedom I would have in creating a design. Still, I jumped at the opportunity to become involved, and today, in light of the pleasure my client derives from the completed work, I have no regrets—actually, I suppose I do have a few regrets and these have yet to be resolved.

The basic issue has to do with compromise. Is it more courageous to listen and respond to the client, or remain unyielding in standing behind some ideal, perfect creation? As a professional who takes some pride in making the people I serve happy, I routinely compromise to some degree—perhaps the use of one color or finish over another. Until this project, I had never compromised on the core of a design concept. Assuming that it was sufficiently strong and clear, "messaging" details without sacrificing content should be feasible. At any rate, this was the philosophy I took into my first meeting with Jim James, anchorman.

One other variable in the compromise equation of this project was the novelty and importance of the work as my first house— a completely new, big building. To have this successfully executed project under my belt would be a notable credential. It is essential to refer to past experience to be taken seriously and to go after similar projects. So, it would not be unreasonable to assert that I was more likely to be "flexible" in the service of designing the James house.

"Traditional home styles are preferred by three out of four respondents," I read with a sinking feeling from parts of a survey published in the *USA Today* I had picked up before boarding the flight to Orlando. Though I was grateful and even gleeful about the prospect of authoring a building, I still hoped I would have some freedom to design something really creative. At least, a semitropical setting presented a very different environment for me, and Mr. James was a rare and different type in his own right. As we descended into the haze of central Florida, I was, however, decidedly uneasy about what lay ahead.

I rented a car at the airport and headed to my first meeting with Jim, at the Dolphin, one of the new Disney hotels. The familiar voice was even more resonant than it was on television: "You must be the one I had Julie hire, it's Andrew, right? I remember the interview I did with your brother, what was it, a year ago, after that plane crash out at O'Hare, yup, he had good advice for those poor families of the dead."

When we finally finished with the protracted greetings and introductions, we got down to business. Jim James had photographs of neighborhood houses that he admired; he wanted a large, "contemporary-traditional." The house was to serve not only as his occasional winter home, but as a year-round getaway for the entire James clan. This rather impressive extended family included James' brother Jerry who had three young children, a wife, a nanny, and a car dealership. The last element had something to do with a requirement for a three-car garage and on-site space for two or three other vehicles.

I returned home worried that I would design something that would be antithetical to anything Jim James would approve. I imagined a voice from *The Fountainhead*—of Roark's mentor—who warns him about the course ahead:

> One day, you'll see on a piece of paper before you a building that will make you want to kneel; you won't believe that you've done it; then you'll think that the earth is beautiful and the air smells of spring and you love your fellow men.... And you'll set out...to have it erected...but only hear your voice begging him, pleading, your voice licking his knees, you'll loathe yourself for it, but you won't

care, if only he'd let you put up that building...you'll want to rip your insides open to show him, because if he saw what's there he'd have to let you put it up. But he'll say that he's very sorry, only the commission has just been given to Guy Francon.... That's your future, Howard Roark. Now, do you want it?

In what I always regarded as not too much more than a cynical gothic romance, the two pages containing the mentor's soliloquy took on a power and meaning I had not previously appreciated. My concern began to grow into anxiety and then raw fear.

How do you hold back, how do you compromise, how do you put all of yourself behind an effort that isn't you, or, like Roark, do you simply not do it at all—or maybe you dynamite the completed work if it has been tainted? This was not the way to sit at my board and start sketching.

I was blocked, frozen by the gravity of all I had to do, by all the potentials of a first house, and by all the limitations in a task that was very much "real world." At this point, my associate came into the picture. Like the good psychologist/physician he is, Peter knows when to deliver a kick. He was not only unsympathetic, but virtually ignored my tortured self-examination. The only thing he said after listening to my own soliloquy was, "Wanna play some tennis?" When this failed to elicit the desired response, he gave me the kick: "Andy, someday you'll have played the game long enough and well enough to have a chance to contribute the way you want to; in the meantime, as the folks at Nike say, 'Just do it'. Call me when you feel like hitting a few—my backhand needs work." Actually he doesn't have a backhand and never will, but I believe he was right about me and the greater scheme of things. *Perhaps it is the very tension between practical exigencies and ideals that motivates innovation and keeps creativity tied to the solution of mundane but significant problems.*

Bold lines on yellow trace form bubbles of primitive spaces that echo the requirements of Jim James. Diagrams take shape, now superimposed on the site plan. An occasional moment of inspiration leaps in with remembrance of a house designed by Frank Lloyd Wright, Charles Moore, or Richard Meier. The process of finding your way into a scheme is not linear or logical, and it is different each time you do it. The initial graphic compositions may have little to do with the final design solution, but may serve as a foundation for further exploration that does yield a key. Then when you think you've wrestled something out of your soul and expressed it on paper, you build a model. Chipboard, Elmer's glue, scissors; rip it apart, change something, rebuild it—for me, this is the architecture of architecture.

FIGURE 3-5
A napkin sketch (top) and the built project (bottom) represent alternative schemes. Common to both is a response to specific site factors: A series of hip roofs cascade down from a height of thirty feet (above the family room) to nine feet (at the garage level). The smaller roofs face the street, and echo the scale and character of adjacent houses. Sketch by Andy Pressman; photo © Dan Forer.

FIGURE 3-6

This series of photos reveal the grand family room as focal point of the design. The skylit double-height volume is at once airy and light-filled, and secure and intimate with its framework of columns, half-wall, and step-down. A second-story bridge that rings the family room serves as a dynamic connection of the master bedroom suite in one wing with the childrens' bedrooms in another. Photos © Dan Forer.

My associate and I were back at Fred's Place, this time with chef's salads and Evian water (as we gradually aged with the practice, we became health conscious). I talked about the project as Peter listened, nodding occasionally. My client, Jim James, was very much on my mind. He was a man who knew exactly what he wanted; I didn't elicit or detect anything other than what he dictated, and if I had some insight, he would not have heard my thoughts on the matter. I was an instrument, a tool for translating Jim's vision into a form acceptable to the building department. That I ended up putting heart, soul, and experience into the translation meant that it was special, professional, even though it was not a work of art.

While I knew that the design was not novel enough to merit coverage in one of the major journals, I was nevertheless satisfied with the work. Orchestrating the players was no small victory: The client insisted on major design changes late in the process (and even considered abandoning the project for a completed builder-home), and the contractor made unilateral decisions without appropriately consulting me. In spite of these hurdles, the house reflects a sensitivity to the client's needs and preferences, and region-specific characteristics of the site, climate, context, and construction techniques.

FIGURE 3-7

The "L"-shaped floor plans of the new 6500 square foot house present narrow masses to facilitate cross ventilation, and wrap around a screen enclosed pool and deck. Rooms have inviting views into the pool area, promoting observation of children at play. Design and drawings by Andy Pressman.

FIGURE 3-8
Deep overhangs (left) reduce solar gain, and tall palms (right) provide shade without blocking breezes at window level. Photos © Dan Forer.

A Collaborative Ideal

Bill Lam is not only a renowned lighting designer (based in Cambridge, MA) but he is a consummate politician in jobs in which the client assumes an active role. What does this really mean? In many of his firm's more than 2000 projects, he has demonstrated success at educating clients about the benefits of good design. I asked Lam to elaborate on his team design process and to generalize about the roles of architects, clients, and consultants.

Client Input
"Take advantage of the client as a significant design resource," says Lam. "Sometimes there are wonderful suggestions and the

design evolves into a better project." He enlists people as allies and collaborators in the design process, simultaneously educating them about time-honored design principles. Designers should *want* to make changes and disregard preconceptions if the project can be improved. Lam cited an example in which a client (the Boston Public Library) made the designers aware of historically important inscriptions that are sculpted into the frieze of the existing building. In the daytime, they are visible but not generally noticed. Rather than illuminate the façade uniformly, Lam aimed lights directly at the inscriptions, which now, for the first time, invite passers-by to read them.

"If a client has a bad idea, we may still try it in model or mock up form, or find a similar built example to analyze. If our own reasoning is sound, we should be able to demonstrate that a poor solution is indeed bad—to the satisfaction of the client." Lam is quite frank about his methods to keep clients not only invested in the project but excited. Obviously, the client's support is critical to the success of any project. Moreover, Lam implores designers to accept the premise that most clients (the real users, owners, and decision makers) are sophisticated and should be able to understand the rationale behind design decisions. Architects have a responsibility to communicate clearly, and he says that this forces the designer to really know what he or she is talking about. According to Lam, clients should simply not accept the attitude, "Believe me because I am a great designer." Rather, the architect's attitude should be, "I'm not doing it my way, I'm doing it *our* way." Accountability for design decisions should be of paramount concern. Lam believes that "Clients should be wary of designers who do not want to listen to them, who would rather be secretive about the design process, and who only present their completed proposals rather than discuss alternatives with a preference articulated. The best client is a strong client who is also willing to listen."

Design by Team

Lam advocates a team approach to preliminary design, and refers to the Caudill Rowlett Scott concept of "squatters" in which client, architect, engineering consultants, and other specialists meet at the site to brainstorm. Values are clarified and design ideas are developed. Perhaps most important for complex projects, systems integration is facilitated with explicit multidisciplinary collaboration resulting from the face-to-face interactions.

This bit of extra work up front promotes efficiency during the design development and construction documents phases, and a better project overall. There are inevitably fewer reversals of concepts at later stages.

On numerous occasions, Lam has challenged mechanical engineers, for example, during these early team meetings, to innovate. It is clear that integrated concepts cannot evolve successfully without the participation of all relevant disciplines. In Lam's experience, structural engineers are typically the most cooperative in working with architects, but they, too, have preconceptions about framing given a certain configuration and size of a building. What the "good ones" share is a desire for excellence; given the motivation and a shared vision of project objectives—that require designing in a nontraditional manner—they *will* collaborate in moving toward this end.

With the right mix of personalities, the team approach to design can be quite synergistic. Lam describes the ideal session:

> In most of the major projects that I've done involving complicated building systems, the essence of the design is created in the first meeting. It is enormously gratifying to be able to engage all of these people and reach agreement. We don't dismiss the design session until everyone is satisfied with their portion of the work. It does, however, require the best qualified people, and those who can make decisions on behalf of their respective offices. These jobs are 10 percent inspiration, 90 percent perspiration, and after an exciting meeting, there is still much work to accomplish. Therefore, rapport and sensitivity among individuals is essential so that meaningful dialogue can continue. An individual has to care more about results than his or her ego. The ideal client participant here is the real user, owner, or decision maker.

Lectures and Field Trips

The lecture and field trip are Lam's one–two punch for educating his clients, which he views as an essential first step to develop a consensus about what constitutes a good building. Only then can the principles be applied to the particular project, and be fully appreciated. Lam says that it is crucial for all the key players, including clients and consultants, to meet at the same time and develop a common language and shared values.

The field trip is typically a critical exploration of both good and bad buildings (mostly bad) that includes visits to Lam's projects. Clients are usually favorably predisposed to appreciat-

FIGURE 3-9
Washington Metropolitan Area Transit Authority illuminated presentation model of a typical subsurface station. Lighting effects were simulated with custom-made lengths of neon tube. Lam says, "Inexpensive study models [such as this one] are one of the most economical means of generating productive discussion within the design team itself." William Lam Associates (lighting consultant), photo courtesy of Harry Weese Associates.

ing them, reports Lam. Clients say, "That's the kind of building we want to build." Selling and educating are dramatically *intertwined*. Moreover, the field trip serves to generate enthusiasm, overcome preconceptions, and develop an understanding of innovative design ideas—in a relatively short period of time.

FIGURE 3-10
*The Rosslyn Station of the
Washington Metro. Bill
Lam's lighting system design
integrates beautifully with
the structure and
furnishings. The brightly
illuminated ceiling vault
counteracts the effect of
subterranean gloom, and
minimizes feelings of
claustrophobia and visual
noise. Photo courtesy of the
Washington Metropolitan
Area Transit Authority.*

The lecture with accompanying slides reinforces the learning in the field with the theoretical underpinnings and rationale of the specific design features. Lam talks about everything from what a good environment means to construction details. He adjusts comments to relate to the local experience. For example, he will take slides of buildings on the way from the airport to the client's office to illustrate principles. And Lam will utilize the lunch break for a minitour of familiar buildings to examine concepts and details. Lam attributes much of his success in dealing with clients to these lectures given at the beginning of projects.

The scale of the project and the design budget will modify but not eliminate Lam's collaborative approach. With small scale work, his involvement is concomitantly reduced, perhaps involving only the development of concepts following a one-hour rather than one-day field trip. He feels that work in the residential arena, for example, is a huge, largely untapped market for this sort of professional consultation.

Bill Lam's greatest strength and satisfaction lies in guiding the design process—the manner in which he educates clients, and describes and then solves problems. While there are many common elements across the body of his work, each project reflects the unique characteristics of his client constituted by the makeup of the design team (those architects/engineers that retain him), and the particular circumstance. Lam clearly enjoys opinionated clients who are not shy about expressing their preferences and requirements. He feels that direct client involvement forms the basis of an appropriate design response along with his own values and personal style. This is what distinguishes Bill Lam and his work—and makes him both a great designer and politician.

Working with Specialty Consultants[1]

Gary Siebein writes about the need for architects (as well as their clients) to recognize situations in which an engineering specialist would be invaluable to collaborate on design. Smart politics means that the architect, as leader of the team, surrounds him- or herself with appropriate experts. Architects are not educated to know everything; the issue of retaining consultants is not a question of dimin-

---

1. An Acoustical Consultant's Perspective. © Gary W. Siebein, 1994.

ishing the role of the architect or losing power, it is very much part of managing a complex process.

Gary W. Siebein is a registered architect, and is principal consultant with Siebein Associates, Consultants in Architectural Acoustics. He is also Professor and Director of the Architecture Technology Research Center, which specializes in architectural acoustics at the University of Florida.

"Technology has reached the stage where buildings no longer fall down: But they are often inconvenient and uncomfortable because the well-known laws of nineteenth-century physics have been ignored well into the twentieth-century."
                    –Cowan, Henry. *An Historical Outline*
                            of Architectural Science. Elsevier
                                Publishing Company, Amsterdam:
                                                1965.

Scene 1: Who's That Knocking on My Floor?

We were hired by a condominium association to undertake field testing and expert witness work for a large, luxurious complex on a beautiful barrier island in south Florida. The condominiums had sold for $250,000 to $500,000 each. They were initially provided with a bare concrete slab for a finish floor, and the Condominium Articles prepared by the developer prior to sales stated that carpet would be installed throughout the building. Many owners did not like carpet. They wanted to install handmade tiles from Mexico, marble from Italy, exotic wood flooring from the rapidly vanishing rain forests, and other beautiful, expensive, difficult-to-install and *noisy* flooring materials in their units. This is usually not a problem in the large single family homes in which many of these owners had previously lived. They hear only themselves walking up stairs. Many were not prepared for the realities of condominium living. The owners complained:

- ❖ "The guy upstairs walks across the floor with his damn golf shoes at five o'clock every morning. It sounds like he's walking in my unit."
- ❖ "The couple two floors up goes out dancing all the time. They come home and who knows what they do up there but her high heels make quite a racket."

❖ "Why does anyone take a shower in the middle of the night? It sounds like Niagara Falls down here when someone upstairs flushes the toilet."

The building formed an efficient, continuous sound distribution system for the footsteps on the floor, the sliding of furniture, and the vibration of plumbing pipes. The case settled out of court. The lawyers for all parties involved probably each own a new Jaguar; the architect, developer, and contractor will face an increase in their liability insurance premiums; and the people living in the buildings will probably never undertake the extensive, disruptive work needed to actually make the renovations to solve the noise problems.

SCENE 1 LESSON.
(1) Let the buyer beware. (2) Listen to buildings; they will speak to you. (3) Architect: Think of the users of the building.

Scene 2: Do People Really Want to *Hear* in an Auditorium?
"We spoke to the architect and he said that providing good acoustics was not within his scope of work for the project."
"What do you mean?" I responded.
My new client elaborated: "We called him because we felt he should fix this. I mean it's awful—we can't understand a word that's said in the room. He said that he designed the building, not how it sounds. That was not in our contract, it's an extra service. He didn't tell us anything about this while we were working on the project. We just want to get it fixed. We *can't* use the room the way it is.
"I think we can help," I added reassuringly.
The committee chair, in disbelief, acknowledged that his group had a brand new building that had to be renovated before it could be used for its intended purposes.
This is how my conversation began with the chairman of the building committee of a community center with a 500 seat multipurpose auditorium with a small stage. He was calling for advice on how to make his recently completed building usable (not perfect, just usable). I met him the following week during a site visit. The building was beautiful but technically deficient.
"What do you use this room for?" I asked.
"Tonight we've got bingo. The people sit right there at the center of the stage with a microphone on the table. On Friday, we're going to have a pot-luck dinner; on Saturday, we've got a

local dance band performing on stage; and a new church is thinking of renting the room on Sunday mornings until they build a building of their own." He continued, "People can't hear very well in the building at all. It sounds all garbled, one word runs into the next. What causes this? Why does it sound so bad?"

"It's really no mystery," I said. "The high ceiling, hard building materials, and angled side wall panels create a long period of reverberation in the room. When someone speaks from the stage, the sound reverberates from every surface in the room for well over two seconds. Each syllable persists in the room long after it is spoken. This is the same thing that happens to a greater extent in a large cathedral."

I had to resist my university professor's habit of delivering a lecture on every subject discussed from explaining the historical significance of the experiments of Wallace Sabine, a young professor at Harvard, in the late 1800s who first quantified this phenomenon and established the scientific basis for architectural acoustics. Sabine was actually presented with a room with similar acoustical problems by the president of the university, and was asked to improve its acoustical qualities. As an untenured young instructor, he worked diligently for over five years in an ambitious experimental program. He would take seat cushions from the theater across the street and place them on the walls and ceiling of the room. He would sound an organ pipe and measure with his stop watch how long the sound reverberated in the room after the organ pipe stopped. He would work late at night so the sounds of the street cars and other city noises would not disturb his work. Each night he would add more cushions or put them in different locations in the room. He was finally able to determine the relationship between the persistence of sound in the room and the amount of seat cushions in the room. We know this quality as reverberation time.

I added, "When the room is used for dinners, sound from people talking to each other at the tables builds up in the large volume of the room so that they probably end up shouting back and forth. The more people there are, the louder they talk. As it gets louder in the room, they talk even more loudly so they can be heard over the din. They are also probably distracted by sounds from other tables reflecting from the angled ceiling surfaces. These sounds compete with their own conversations and disorient them as to the location and content of their dialogues."

Should the acoustical qualities of the room be the responsibility of the architect? No one asked us; but our answer would have been a resounding *yes!* The acoustical qualities of rooms are a direct result of their architectural design: The shape, materials, volume, and so on all influence the sound of the room. It was the architect's responsibility to either deal with these issues herself or to engage the services of a specialty consultant to assist in these matters.

Unfortunately, many of these problems could not be corrected at the stage of the project when we were first consulted—only symptomatic improvements could be made. An extensive diagnostic procedure involving field measurements and computer simulations identified problem surfaces and materials in the room. The sound system was redesigned. Several months later, after this additional work was completed, the community had a building they could use and enjoy. During the initial design, had someone considered that people may actually want to hear each other in an auditorium, an even better room could have been built for less money, and the community could have been using it all along.

SCENE 2 LESSON.
Too often, specialty consultants are not part of the design team for many projects. Acoustics are considered only in "problem" buildings such as open plan offices, factories, hotels near airports, and so on, or in special buildings such as radio stations and theaters.

Every building has an acoustical environment that is designed as the building is designed. Sometimes this is designed with specific intentions and sometimes it is left to chance. When it is left to chance, the results are usually less than satisfactory. Look for specialty consultants to help the owner, users, and designers achieve the goals to which they aspire on each project. A carefully chosen consultant will complement the assets the owner and the architect bring to the project.

Most important, learn to know what you do not know! In other words, be keenly aware of situations that require additional assistance in a specialty discipline even on seemingly simple projects such as the one described above.

Scene 3: The Vacuum Cleaner Analogy

"If it doesn't make a lot of noise, people won't think it cleans" (anonymous vacuum cleaner salesman when asked by the author if a quieter model was available).

The building was completed. The contractor wanted to receive a Certificate of Substantial Completion. The owner would not accept the building because of excessive noise from the heating, ventilating, and air conditioning system in all rooms. This problem took five years of design and construction to create. The owner expected an "expert" from out of town to come in and solve the extensive noise problems in five days with little cost and no modifications to the building so they could move in right away.

SCENE 3 LESSON.
You don't have to hear it to be cool. A frustrating part of a consultant's work is the renovation of recently completed buildings to meet the expectations of owners and users of the buildings under very tense situations.

The role of the consultant and the probable success of the project are severely compromised in these situations. The retrofits are expensive and time consuming. Walls that have already been built are taken down. New walls are built. The building cannot be used for some periods of time. The results are never the same as if the issues had been considered within the context of the total design solution from the beginning; and they are always more expensive.

Doing It the Right Way From the Beginning

A much preferred role is for the consultant to be involved with the design team from the beginning of the project. Often, acoustical design concepts, if discussed during programming or in a schematic design meeting, can result in simple changes to a design that can improve the acoustical qualities of the building and also improve the overall design with little or no cost. The consultant's participation in job meetings is essential. A specialty consultant can translate the qualitative statements of the owner or user into design criteria, organizational concepts, and building systems that can be used in the design of the building.

During design development, the consultant works to implement these goals in planning and zoning the building in concept, preliminary selection of construction assemblies, preliminary design of sound systems and other equipment, participate in budget reviews and value engineering (cost cutting) meetings, and provide a general review of the overall architectural and engineering scheme to ensure that it meets the programmed intentions.

During the construction documents phase, the consultant will produce special details where required, specify sound system and other specialty equipment, continue participation in budget reviews, and review the work of the rest of the design team so that the total building package will meet the design criteria and concepts formed during programming and schematic design.

Construction administration is also necessary from the consultant's perspective. Meeting with the contractors who will perform sound insulation details is helpful to teach them the importance of attention to the details of sealing and penetrations in walls, floors, and so on.

Architects will frequently wait until the construction documents phase to engage a consultant. They mistakenly think this will save some of their hard earned fee for themselves. Unfortunately, the results are often more time consuming for all involved because the design scheme must be substantially revised late in the process. It is also embarrassing for an architect to approach a client shortly before bid date with organizational revisions to an already accepted scheme that are required to solve acoustical problems.

In summary, learn to work productively with consultants as important members of the design team. Don't try to save money by waiting until late in the design process to hire consultants who will then be unable to satisfy the needs of the project. Hire the consultants for full services for programming through construction administration. Listen to the consultant's recommendations carefully, especially regarding the necessary scope of work and the difficult trade-offs that are often required between the many complex factors in every architectural project.

CHAPTER 4

FOREIGN AFFAIRS

Globalization of architecture has become a reality: American firms are following their clients and designing buildings all over the world. And just as American businesses are expanding internationally, so too are foreign entities conducting business and requiring facilities in this country. Washington area architect Marvin Cantor tells a once in a lifetime story of a foreign government awarding him a commission to design a chancery in the heart of the District.

A special kind of political understanding and conduct is essential to successful navigation of local ways and customs. Roger K. Lewis writes about his stint in the Peace Corps—also a singular and enlightening experience.

In the first section, Stanley Tigerman has assembled several amazing vignettes from over 30 years of practice. Only the last one is a foreign affair. The other three are set stateside, but are sufficiently exotic that they earned a place in this section.

Emotion and Ethics in Architecture

Perhaps one of the most thoughtful and reflective architects of our time, Stanley Tigerman, FAIA, has written and built extremely provocative work worldwide. He was more than a little upset with what he perceived to be a negative connotation in the theme of The

Fountainheadache. *Tigerman has said that* The Fountainhead *was and continues to be influential in his life. It is the heroism of going against the grain that motivates him to sometimes outrageous and often noble goals, as he illustrates below.*

Tigerman is a partner, with his wife, in the Chicago-based architecture firm Tigerman McCurry. He has taught widely in the United States and abroad; he has written four books including The Architecture of Exile *(1988); and there have been numerous books and articles on his award-winning projects.*

We all have war stories, horror stories, wonderful stories about clients, situations, buildings—things that we've been engaged with as architects. But rather than dwell on, as you called it, "The Fountainheadache" side of things—architecture is too optimistic for me to find "downers" or even worse, ways of mocking situations and so forth. So I would rather just tell you a whole bunch of vignettes of the *really good* things that have happened to me because, for me, these 30-plus years that I've been in my own practice have *not* been a "Fountainheadache." They are actually a fulfillment of the raw, unbridled optimism that I always saw in the book *The Fountainhead.*

Two projects that have wonderful stories associated with them occurred fairly early in my practice, and involved remodelling barns into houses. The first barn, in Wisconsin, was done for a couple who had inherited a piece of land near Burlington, WI that had a barn on it. They came to me to remodel the barn into a house. I did. They loved it. They spent a lot of time there; they lived in Chicago, but it was a weekend house for them.

Over time, in one of life's tragedies, she contracted an incurable disease very prematurely in her life. Then, the most remarkable thing happened. As she began to disintegrate, she still looked terrific, but her husband, knowing that she was going to die, started to lose weight, became increasingly morose, and generally looked terrible. Everyone around him knew (and certainly as the architect, I knew) what was happening.

The woman did an extraordinary thing, right out of a movie from the late 1930s or early 1940s with Myrna Loy in which she played the part of a woman who was dying. Her husband, who loved her very much, started to go to pieces. Seeing this, she fixed him up with their daughter's piano teacher, making sure that the teacher was invited to various dinners and was seated next to her husband—while the wife was still alive. There was a kind of transition between the wife and this other woman—a passing of the baton.

It worked in the movie. It worked in real life too, because the wife, observing her husband deteriorate, found a young woman colleague whom she situated in proximity to her husband. At one point when her condition was irredeemable, the wife took a one-way plane trip to Switzerland, checked into a hospice, and died with dignity. Sure enough, the husband, as he experienced this tragedy, became closer to this young woman, and they ultimately married. This is the kind of story that I like.

The second story involves another barn conversion in Michigan that I did in the late 1960s/early 1970s. It was actually one of the nicest projects I had ever done for two of the very nicest people I have ever known. We got along wonderfully—they were fabulous clients.

When the job was finished, I came to my office one day and there was a big crate from them with a little envelope—a bread and butter thank you note. I opened the crate, and it was a case of 1936 Chateau Lafite-Rothschild, which in 1970 was worth a ton of money. The note said how unhappy they were now that this was all finished and they were disappointed that we just could not continue. This is the kind of story that I frankly cherish!

FIGURE 4-1
Barn conversion into a weekend retreat in Burlington, WI for a Chicago couple (1969–1972). Section-perspective drawing courtesy of Stanley Tigerman.

You see, for me, architecture is the kind of discipline wherein you are supposed to bring joy to people. When they respond and correspondingly return that joy to the architect, those are the sort of things I choose to remember. I'm not sure that I would want to relate so-called horror stories. Books are read by lots of people and rather than be amusing and clever, considering that some young person might pick up a book like this, I would want some stories (albeit perhaps in the minority) of at least one architect who gave and received a lot of joy. So if there is a legacy that I'm going to leave, I would want others to follow in those footsteps. We are supposed to bring each other joy in this world. And architecture is one of those things that can actually do it. You can create pain and difficulties, or you can create joy. It's not that my life or my practice is problem free, but this business of the architect playing the villain—the arrogant bastard—who is arcane and does not communicate is not my idea of architecture.

Another story involves a guy who came to me in the middle 1970s wanting to do a house in Indiana in the Dunes. He was crude and crass, and he owned strip joints in Calumet City and formerly in Key West. More impressively, he recently had a double colostomy, which was the manifestation of terminal intestinal cancer. He wanted to build a house for himself and his wife and two daughters. I thought that was fabulous. I didn't know

FIGURE 4-2
"Frog Hollow," barn/ house conversion in Berrien Springs, MI (1973–1974). Sketch by Stanley Tigerman.

what to do in the beginning. I didn't know how to handle it. Nobody ever came to me to do a house when they were dying, for God's sake. I ultimately came to realize that this was wonderful (talk about optimism!). It was a constructive act of a person, who even if he knew exactly how far down the tunnel the light was, nonetheless was going to go out in a blast. So what do you do for a guy like that? What kind of house do you do?

I designed this vulgar, so-called "pornographic" house that I took a great deal of joy in doing because *it made the guy laugh,* and that was the point of it. It brought a lot of joy to him at the end of his life. He was difficult—aren't we all?—he knew he was dying. He was very demanding. But this house really made him happy: It was erotic; it was shaped like an erect phallus with semen coming out the end as steps cascading down the hill. But the house had a certain "stylishness" that was almost therapeutic, if you can imagine such a thing. He loved recounting what that house meant, and the fact that it made him chuckle. That's the kind of stuff, as far as I'm concerned, that's really important to do.

Sometimes what you do as an architect and as a person that is really important is at a much larger level or scope. For example, for a period of 10 years, I worked on a series of polytechnic institutes in what is now Bangladesh, but I began the project when it was East Pakistan. I worked collaboratively with a wonderful man who was my classmate in my Masters program at Yale in 1961.

As all young people in graduate school often do when they are really good friends albeit half-way around the world from each other, we swore that we would find some way to spend more time and work together. Sure enough, he structured a situation that brought me to Dacca in 1964 through the vehicle of the World Bank, which was in the process of funding these five vocational training institutes in five jungle villages with the government of East Pakistan.

The years passed. In 1971, our five projects were under construction in the five different locations. In 1971, the struggle for liberation in East Pakistan began against Islamabad and what was then West Pakistan to attain independence in what has since has become the People's Republic of Bangladesh. During the course of that struggle, my friend had been instrumental in engaging in dialogue with a certain Sheik, using his office as a

FIGURE 4-3

*"Daisy House," a private
residence in Porter, IN
(1975–1978). Entrance
axonometric drawing
courtesy of Stanley
Tigerman.*

place to coalesce ideas and even to foment revolution. I was witness to many of these proceedings.

When the actual war began, I was back in Chicago and I started getting correspondence from our various site offices of what the revolution really meant with respect to the projects. One of the workers was killed, several of the staff at different sites were beaten-up by the Pakistan Army, and so forth. I decided that I couldn't engage in that any longer, so I wrote a letter to my classmate, who by then had fled to Calcutta. I said that I thought I was going to resign the commission because I couldn't maintain the kind of distance you have to maintain working for a government—West Pakistan—which was in the process of reducing East Pakistan to an agricultural land by killing the intellectuals by genocide.

I then founded the Bangladesh Defense League, I raised money for guns for Bangladesh, and finally, in September 1971, I went to Dacca and I told our Pakistani client that I just couldn't continue any more, that I was very upset, and that I was going to resign the commissions. I took a plane to Bangkok and then doubled-back to Calcutta to see my classmate, who had arranged a press conference. I resigned. I said that it wasn't my role nor that of any architect to structure situations in which people who are employed by me are killed as a part of another agenda. I added that I hoped that when Bangladesh became a free state I could finish the projects.

By December of that year and into January 1972, it finally became an independent Bangladesh. One of the first acts that transpired was to get me reappointed. But the World Bank (I think under pressure from the U.S. government) had not liked the fact that I had resigned, in other words, that I had become, to use their term, "political." They resisted my reappointment. But in any case, the People's Republic of Bangladesh prevailed, and I was in fact reappointed.

I finished the projects, and there are two postscripts that are very interesting in my view: One is an "upper" and one a "downer;" one occurred almost immediately and one occurred practically yesterday. The upper happened in 1974 when I went back for my last trip to see the projects inhabited and participate in a bunch of ceremonies announcing the beginning of the operations of the polytechnic institutes. I'll never forget in Pabna, on one of the sites where a ceremony was taking place, a young boy, a student who had no arms and had only one leg, presented me with a plaque for my courage in speaking out on their behalf. Mind you, I was able-bodied—he was practically destroyed by that war, and he was congratulating *me*. You can imagine the emotion that I felt.

The downer occurred recently when a professor of urban planning from Calcutta came to Chicago in 1993 to invite me to a conference there. He had actually invited me two years earlier but presumably because of the Persian Gulf war, the conference was postponed, or, in any case, the funding from the USIA was curtailed using the rationale of the Gulf war. This gentleman told me, just recently, that the reason that my funding didn't

FIGURE 4-4
Five polytechnic institutes, Bangladesh (1964–1974). Site axonometric drawing courtesy of Stanley Tigerman.

come through was because the U.S. government did not want me to go back because they felt that I had been "political."

If these stories are useful, maybe they stand in counterpoint to others who will be happier to tell horror stories and war stories in their practice and in their career. I think architecture is obligated to try to heal, to put Humpty-Dumpty back together again. These little vignettes are examples of many more that I could tell you. They are very important in understanding how these experiences have shaped my belief in a moral and ethical basis that underpins a discipline like architecture. If that basis does not exist, there really is no promise in something that is detached from human emotion. Architecture is supposed to reinforce those human emotions and our optimistic belief in the perpetuation of the species—not our belief in the bomb. I think it is a field that, at its best, ignites passion from a moral and ethical foundation.

A Project Dies Because a Country Disappears

Marvin J. Cantor, FAIA, has been a principal in private practice since 1960 in the Washington, DC region. His clients have included many foreign governments for projects related to their operations and activities in the District of Columbia. Mr. Cantor has been honored by the American Institute of Architects with many leadership and service awards. Also noteworthy is his sense of humor, that in no small way must account for his success and longevity in the profession.

In Mr. Cantor's following tale about the design of a chancery for a foreign government, worldwide political events collide with the politics of the architect–client relationship. The message here is that while two parties may communicate and compromise quite ideally, there are forces over which no one has control, and these will occasionally determine the fate of any project.

We have all heard the stories of projects failing because of the client's inability to secure financing, the city's zoning board denying a sought-after variance, the market demand drying-up, and so on. But how often does a project evaporate because the client, a sovereign nation, disappears from the world map? This is one such story in a lifetime.

By 1981, the German Democratic Republic (GDR), popularly known as East Germany, had logged diplomatic relations with the United States for over 20 years. East German officials decided it was time to investigate moving out of an eighth-floor office rental space in downtown Washington, DC and into an impressive new chancery building ("as would befit a first-class sovereign country") in the international center of Washington. Accordingly, the office of Marvin J. Cantor, FAIA, Architect was retained to start preliminary planning for this effort. The start was auspicious, but shortly thereafter, a combination of world events brought the project to a standstill: The Soviet occupation of Afghanistan, the increasingly harsh enforcement of the Berlin Wall barricade ... the cold war heated-up, and international relations with the Eastern Block sunk to the barest minimum short of breaking-off diplomatic relations. The project entered a deep freeze!

In 1985, a fresh breeze blew into the Soviet Union. Mikhail Gorbachev became the country's new leader, and embarked on his famous policy of glasnost and perestroika. In 1986, Gorbachev paid a visit to President Reagan, taking time off to stop his motorcade on Connecticut Avenue and shake hands with DC citizens, and a new era of "friendship" with the Eastern

Block countries began. Early 1987 brought renewed interest in the GDR proposed chancery, and once again, Cantor's office began the planning process. This time, however, following a period of international unrest that had terrorists targeting all types of establishments, with embassies and chanceries heading the list, the GDR foreign office supplied what it felt was an appropriate architectural solution to its Washington Chancery (see Figure 4-5).

The fortress-like, mausoleum quality of the design could not be overlooked, and Cantor, realizing that the Washington, DC Office of Planning, the National Capitol Planning Commission, and the Commission on Fine Arts would all eventually have to approve the project, immediately turned the proposed design down indicating that it, "Just would not fly in DC." Instead, he came up with a new design (see Figure 4-6) that resolved the problem of security for the sensitive offices while maintaining an open and inviting "office building" type of exterior that would still possess the monumentality a foreign country might like to achieve in its proposed new mission outpost.

The design was essentially a square doughnut organization with the most sensitive offices opening from a central atrium, and protected around the outer perimeter of the building by corridors and nonsensitive spaces. The vertical circulation and service cores were located at the building corners whose windowless facades served to anchor the building and provide the grand scale that the clients demanded.

From early 1987 until late 1989, the planning process moved forward; the government agencies mentioned earlier had all

FIGURE 4-5
Preliminary design sketch of the proposed Chancery developed by the German Democratic Republic's foreign office.

FIGURE 4-6
Design of the proposed Chancery of the German Democratic Republic in Washington, DC by the office of Marvin J. Cantor, FAIA, Architect of Fairfax, VA. Rendering by Hossein Rashtian.

given the green light to the preliminary designs, and construction documents were then started, and finally completed in early 1990.

But, in November 1989, the Berlin Wall came down! How, why, and when are subjects that will occupy historians for decades to come, but the inescapable fact was that the wall came down! Now talk of future unification of East and West Germany started to emanate from both countries; however, without question this would be years, even decades into the future. At a diplomatic reception in December 1989, when then GDR Ambassador Gerhardt Herder was asked about it, his reply (roughly paraphrased) was, "It will be a long arduous process; we are two separate people with two distinctly separate forms of governments, two different ideologies, and dramatically different responsibilities for World War II (it seems that all of the unrepentant Nazis went to West Germany, and all that was left in East Germany were those Germans who never really were in favor of Hitler's policies or actions). Unification is but a "dream," now we must proceed without question on the Chancery to its completion!"

In May 1990 the construction documents were completed, the bid invitations were prepared, and the bidders list was narrowed to those who would be asked to submit prices on the building's construction. All that was necessary was the final United States State Department clearance to issue the plans. However, between January and May of that year, events in the two Germanies were moving with unprecedented speed and surprise! And at the end of May, the earthshaking announcement that the USSR would not oppose the unification process put the final piece of the puzzle in place. Unification had become not only a viable future dream, but an almost immediate reality! No plans were issued, and when East German marks were converted to West German currency on July 1, 1990, the official word came down that the GDR was on its way to extinction. The impressive and detailed model of the building was returned to the architect (where it now resides in silent splendor), the final contractual fees were paid in full (as client, the architect felt that they had behaved in the finest tradition), and the project was consigned to the dustbin of history!

The Hospitable Tunisians

In the first of several intriguing contributions to The Fountainhead-ache, *Roger K. Lewis, FAIA, describes a truly unique and memorable relationship with clients in an international arena.*

Roger K. Lewis is a practicing architect in Washington, DC and a professor of architecture at the University of Maryland. His weekly column, "Shaping the City," appears in The Washington Post. *Professor Lewis authored* Architect? A Candid Guide to the Profession, *published in 1985 by The MIT Press. His projects have received many AIA design awards and have been cited in both the popular and trade press. (His cartoons are a personal favorite of mine, and are scattered throughout* The Fountainheadache.)

Of all the clients I have ever worked with, my favorite were those I served when I was in the Peace Corps in Tunisia.

Just out of architecture school, inexperienced yet eager and self-confident, I spent two formative years—from 1964 to 1966—as a volunteer architect working for the Tunisian Ministry of Public Works.

I was among the first architects stationed in the ministry's regional office in the small town of Nabeul, the seat of government of one of Tunisia's 14 provinces. For many years there had been no architects, private or public, in this region of the country, the North African peninsula reaching northeastwardly toward Sicily. When Tunisia gained its independence from France in 1956, most of the country's French and Italian architects returned to Europe, leaving Tunisia with no one to design buildings. Thus local officials who governed the province and its towns waited enthusiastically, project commissions and funding in hand, for architects to arrive.

Almost weekly, mayors, provincial delegates, and directors of various civic organizations walked into our office and, after the requisite salutations, proceeded to describe their site and what they wanted built on it. Then they departed with the expectation that, within days, the ministry and its youthful American architects would complete the necessary designs, produce construction drawings and cost estimates, and initiate project construction. Sometimes it actually happened this quickly.

In less than two years, I designed more than 30 projects, half of which were either built completely or under construction before I left the country in June 1966.

A special kind of mutual understanding existed between the Peace Corps Volunteer architects and our Tunisian clients. The Tunisians were our hosts as well as the people we served. They had invited us to come there to help them build. Most important, they believed that we had been chosen and sent because we were professional experts, university graduates armed with knowledge and talent, notwithstanding our youth. Our status seemed assured when we were given the exalted title "architecte-urbaniste."

From our simultaneously idealistic and pragmatic perspective, we were there as volunteers, minimally compensated, funded by the American government, able to choose to leave at any time should circumstances warrant. The Tunisians were our clients, but they weren't really paying us. We were committed to living like Tunisians live, not like tourists or diplomats, yet we still were different, still guests. And we knew, and we knew that the Tunisians knew, that we could make proposals, offer advice, and take actions that a Tunisian employed by the ministry never could. We were expected to be polite, but we could be fearlessly candid.

The consequence of this unusual relationship was that we enjoyed remarkable credibility. My Tunisian clients would look at preliminary sketches and, after some explanation and general discussion, ask how soon I could put dimensions on the drawings so the contractor could break ground. After presenting a design, I rarely had to defend it against the usual challenges concerning costs, materials, functional efficiency, or stylistic mannerisms. Never was I asked to explore additional, fruitless alternatives once a design direction was adequately explained and justified. Reasonable aesthetic innovation was welcomed, although certain cultural traditions—for example, buildings always were finished with white stucco—and technical and economic imperatives had to be respected.

Occasionally, a client would voice skepticism about a design idea, usually related to finishes or details. To win them over, I would make a deal. "Build the project as designed and if the outcome proves unsatisfactory, I will gladly authorize changing it." Such an offer was feasible because labor and local materials in Tunisia were inexpensive. The strategy succeeded; no project was changed after it was built.

The usually positive chemistry between me and my Tunisian clients reflected a combination of mutually understood motivations and clarity of means. First, Tunisia's agenda was clear: They needed projects—civic auditoriums, schools, libraries, clinics, public parks, hotels, shopping facilities, housing—designed and built quickly. And they were able to articulate their purposes sufficiently for me to respond, even if I was playing by ear much of the time. Second, available technology was simple and readily mobilized. With limited choices to make, we could focus on basic formal issues of space-making, massing, and structural geometry.

With rare exceptions, Tunisians dealt with me as a professional, believing that I was at least a competent designer and, at best, an inspired one. And in aesthetic matters, my judgment was regularly sought and faithfully carried out. It was the best of times, a time before I had learned that, in the United States, clients are not always so believing or respectful.

CHAPTER 5

IS THE CAMEL A HORSE DESIGNED BY COMMITTEE?

Roger K. Lewis invokes the camel cliché later in this chapter in a scene in which the building committee of an institutional client has retained a weak-willed architect. Howard Roark from *The Fountainhead* would sooner set fire to the camel then let it live in full glory. So, how should architects deal with committees, and vice versa, to produce excellent buildings?

Professor Lewis points out that it is *not sufficient* to meet budget, program, and schedule—you can still end up with a camel. Concern for humanism and client needs are obviously crucial to the success of any project, but, as Robert Marquis has said, they should not be used as an excuse for average or poor work.

It is the architect's *personal relationship* with committee members that can reach beyond the bureaucratic politics that grind design projects toward mediocrity. Leslie Wexner (of Wexner Center for the Visual Arts at Ohio State fame) is a noteworthy patron of architecture. His attitude in working with the best architects is that "Great architecture is produced by great artists, not by lay people who critique and edit the work." Howard Roark would surely agree.

The Client of Many Minds

Roger K. Lewis, FAIA, contributes this incisive piece regarding the myriad interests of design committee members, and the importance of strong leadership on the part of the client in producing high-quality architecture. (The biography for Roger Lewis appears in "The Hospitable Tunisians" in Chapter 4.)

Perhaps the most throbbing kind of headache for architects accompanies designing projects such as schools, hospitals, museums, or churches. Common to this type of client—the public or civic institution—is the existence of a constituency of individuals, each of whom has a legitimate and direct stake in the outcome of the design process. Each also has a legitimate voice but invariably a different point of view about what matters architecturally. Consequently, the architect must try to satisfy often conflicting desires and needs of many: Overseers, administrators, users, members, donors, and the community served. Often the architect works with a building committee, most of whose members have never before built anything.

Like corporate clients, institutions develop their own internal cultures of power and competition, notwithstanding the shared values and goals of the organization's constituents. And the architect must comprehend this internal culture. Yet even when the political landscape of the institution is understood, traversing it unscathed is difficult. No strong architectural advocacy will please everybody. Aesthetic and functional compromises, usually driven by economic and operational considerations, have to be made. Not everyone represented on the building committee will get everything he or she wants.

Not surprisingly, timid or obsequious architects frequently find themselves producing the most mediocre architecture as they struggle to satisfy equally every condition imposed. Given the opportunity, the institutional client—represented by the building committee—will have its way totally, bullying and badgering the architect until it gets a building that responds perfectly to the budget and program, no matter how ugly or poorly detailed the building might be. This is the proverbial camel, a horse designed by a committee.

When institutional architecture achieves aesthetic as well as functional and financial success, it reflects not only skillful work by the architect, but also strong, individual leadership within the institution—by a board or committee chairman, an executive director, a president, or an outspoken and active benefactor. The right kind of wise and inspired leadership brings to the process a compelling vision for the institution, a set of aspirations that can invigorate architecture. These aspirations transcend program and budget. When such leadership exists, the architect's job becomes much easier.

Design with Committees

We know that architects do their best work when the client is a strong, open-minded individual with vision. Architects must also work with design committees. In this interesting discourse by Kent Larson, the anatomy of committee dynamics is presented in explicit terms.

Kent Larson has practiced architecture in New York City since 1980 as partner with Peter L. Gluck and Partners, Architects. He is Partner-in-Charge of much of the private and institutional work of the firm, and writes regularly for Progressive Architecture *and other publications.*

Committees are a fact of life with institutional design projects. It is the rare architect who can play the many roles required to avoid all conflict with a committee *and* make good architecture. In spite of having little or no formal training in group dynamics or communications, the architect must become a hybrid of leader, persuader, arbitrator, creator, improvisor, technical and legal expert, showman, patient listener, and, at times, therapist. Many of the great twentieth-century architects experienced major problems with design committees, lacking one or more of these skills. The best presentations to a group are often more theater than an enumeration of the architectural ideas. It is common for large firms to have front men skilled in the art of presentation—who seldom design and spend most of their time wooing clients, entertaining, and eating lunch.

Each committee situation is unique. Our most complicated process was for the design of a Presbyterian church, with its separate design committee, interior design subcommittee, pipe-organ subcommittee, liturgical committee, stained glass subcommittee, grounds committee, and construction committee. At the other extreme was a no-nonsense group for the design of Columbia University's Graduate School of Business addition who wanted to be involved with only the most major decisions. The most unusual committee experience was a nonlinear process with constantly shifting budget, program, and committee membership for the design of a new synagogue. All had their difficult moments, but the design was, by and large, successful in the end. We have found that it helps to keep a few things in mind while navigating through the logistical, political, and personal mine fields of committee-based architectural design:

- *Motivations Vary:* Members give up valuable family, work, or television time to attend committee meetings, which are often held at night. Most join in the selfless interest of helping a valued institution. Some are reluctant members who just couldn't say no. A few volunteer to gain or exercise power, stroke their egos, or develop contacts with powerful people. Understanding why each person joined a committee is the first step in working successfully with the group.
- *Skills and Interests Are Very Different:* Committee members seem to fall into one of two groups—lawyers and everyone else. Lawyers are often articulate and persuasive, and function well as strategists and spokespeople. They frequently don't have a clue about architecture (and the best will admit this). The rest can range from CEOs to homemakers to architects. The latter are by far the worst to work with because they cannot help but impose their own agenda. Homemakers are often the most sensitive to the subtleties of a design and the most open to new ideas. Some members have only pragmatic planning concerns, some are interested only in controlling the money, some focus on the approval strategy, and some are bored with anything but aesthetic issues. Sometimes a strong leader will emerge who becomes, in effect, the client through the influence over others. This, of course, can go either way—it is all in the luck of the draw.
- *The Path of Least Resistance Is Banality:* Strong ideas will elicit powerful emotional responses pro and con. Weak design work is the easiest to get a committee to approve. Since it is always less risky to oppose something than to support it, the strongest forces will push toward the weakening of an idea—away from anything perceived as unconventional or with rough edges. It seems, however, that opponents of a proposal usually approve the finished product if it remains fundamentally uncompromised. An architect must keep in mind that it is easy to give in, but hard to make good architecture.
- *Prima Donnas Don't Go Far with Committees:* While it is important to keep a design from being undermined, it is the kiss of death to become labeled as an unsympathetic

artist who is unconcerned with the needs and wishes of the client. Good ideas must be adopted without hesitation, and the larger architectural goals must be reinforced over and over. Members can more easily accept the rejection of a suggestion if they understand the design values. Life can be miserable for the architect if an influential committee member is actively opposed to a proposal. An architect should cultivate working relationships with the people of influence on a committee. Make allies not enemies.

❖ *Pick the Battles:* Committee work always involves compromise. A good architect will know when to compromise and when to stand firm. A few inappropriate suggestions must be accepted at times if they do not affect the core elements of a design. In other words, lose the little fights but win the big ones.

❖ *Large Committees Are Often More Manageable:* It is true that a committee of more than five can do little work. Design committees, however, are not formed to do any work, but to review, recommend, and approve. A smaller committee often begins to micromanage the design process, leading to interminable meetings dealing with trivial detail. With a large committee, it is much easier for the architect to call for a vote up or down—and then move on to the next issue. If the matter is critical, however, the architect should be fairly certain of winning. It is difficult to revisit an issue after rejection.

❖ *Use Minutes to Help Control the Process:* Minutes of meetings are one of the great inventions of committee-based architecture. They bring order to the process, focus attention, minimize misunderstandings, and save a great deal of time.

❖ *Make Decisions Stick:* Few committee members make every meeting. Some will expect a recap of previous presentations they missed, in spite of the minutes. Some will arrive late and ask that the meeting begin again for their benefit. On occasion, members will feel that decisions made at meetings they didn't attend (they are always men) are null and void because the group did not benefit from their greater experience. Patience is a virtue in these circumstances, but the process quickly becomes unmanageable, and time is wasted when this becomes a pattern. Rules

FIGURE 5-1
*Addition to Uris Hall,
Graduate School of
Business, Columbia
University. Designing with
a committee* can *produce
excellent results. Kent
Larson, Partner-in-Charge,
Peter L. Gluck and
Partners, Architects. Photo
by Paul Warchol, courtesy
of Peter L. Gluck and
Partners, Architects.*

must be established at the outset to deal with these problems. Rule number one: Those present are empowered to make decisions for those not present.

❖ *Protect Clients from Themselves:* There is a trap that every architect eventually falls into: Certain members will insist that the budget is fixed and can't be exceeded, while others will insist that additional items are absolutely essential regardless of their cost. A committee will rarely come to terms with this contradiction internally—leaving the architect caught in the middle. This is a no win situation, with people upset if expectations must be lowered to meet the budget, and others upset if the budget must be raised to fulfill wishes. The problem is often compounded by an architect's natural inclination to gravitate to the more ambitious scheme, and to optimistically assume that costs will be lower than is realistic. It is far easier to postpone a reckoning than to face it head on, but the price is reduced credibility when reality hits (bids). It must be made clear that a client cannot set the budget *and* the scope *and* the quality of the work. The architect has the responsibility to see that the client takes responsibility for the limitations of their budget. Architects must be many things, but magician is not a required role.

There is no doubt that a building designed with a committee is typically a bit more compromised and less adventurous than other work, but there are unique rewards. Chief among them is the pleasure of working closely with a diverse group of people to turn their seemingly contradictory requirements and wishes into a strong, well-conceived, satisfying solution.

Institutions, Clients, and Service

An integral aspect of functioning in any political scene is the degree to which the constituent publics and special interest groups are identified and served. Norman Rosenfeld, FAIA, describes below the unique nature of services to one such special group—institutional clients—and the committees who represent them.

Mr. Rosenfeld is the founding principal of Norman Rosenfeld, FAIA Architects, a New York City-based architectural firm, since 1969 specializing in the programming, planning, and design for health care, education, and commercial projects. He has lectured widely and taught hospital planning and design courses for graduate students and architects.

Institutional clients are a breed apart. Because health care, educational, and cultural institutions are such complex building types run by multifaceted constituencies of administrators, professionals, and technicians, providing architectural services to these institutions is an extraordinarily demanding professional challenge. This is not a complaint but simply a realistic observation on a very special architect–client niche relationship.

Architects practicing in the institutional field need highly developed skills in a multitude of disciplines. A validation (I am delighted to share) of a successful client relationship is evidenced in this hospital client's reference letter for my firm:

> Norman and his associates are more than architects—they are systems consultants, public relations advisors, historians, mechanics, decorators, designers, and fierce advocates of our hospital's physical plants, which will long survive us all.

FIGURE 5-2
A COMMUNITY GENERAL HOSPITAL
●*Funding needed for facility improvements in a financially distressed hospital.*
This project was planned to improve the antiquated diagnostic and treatment departments of this aging community general hospital. Physician support and patient occupancy were falling off. To finance the capital program, the hospital had to transfer ownership from the City to a voluntary status to access the financial market. The new "front entrance" and radiology, surgery, laboratory, and emergency departments have reversed the hospital's "image" and finances bringing in new physicians and improved health care delivery. Photo by Norman McGrath, courtesy of Norman Rosenfeld, FAIA Architects.

While it does make me blush more than a little, this client understands and values what we try to do. The projects we have done for them have been successful—even the ones not yet built have served the institutional purpose of satisfying the Board and the Medical Staff that Administration is sensitive to facility needs and seeking to improve image, environment, and bottom line. It is enormously rewarding to be an architect in this professional environment where we are called on to satisfy vying needs, to work with bright and dedicated staff, to accommodate requirements for cutting-edge technology, to meet stringent and often conflicting codes, and to ultimately provide an environ-

FIGURE 5-3

A GOVERNMENT HOSPITAL

●*Persistence, patience, and "stay with it" can produce good architecture.*
Government agency clients present unique architect–client relations. This project
extended 10 years from initial contact to completion. The project passed through
three changes of management in the central office and four site facility directors.
Each new participant voiced somewhat different views of the developing project.
At a considerable hardship, the architect, the only constant in the 10-year process,
remained a strong advocate for the integrity of the initial design concepts. Photo
courtesy of Norman Rosenfeld, FAIA Architects.

ment, in this case, for healing, which satisfies staff and patients
and gives us a sense of pride in our practice.

The selection process for institutional architects is complex.
There isn't one entrepreneur CEO who decides. Often it is a
committee process established to ensure representation of many
constituencies. In the final analysis, the selection of an architect
requires a good deal of courage and an equal amount of faith.
After all, an architectural project is among the largest invest-
ments made by an individual, a corporation, or an institution.
The selection of an architect to conceive of and guide this investment is a weighty choice.

Retaining the services of an architect is a unique experience,
even to those institutional leaders who may be accustomed to

"purchasing" all sorts of things. The product of an architect's services is not something you can "kick the tires" or "compare sticker prices" before you buy. Unlike the purchase of an automobile, buyers have little ability to judge the quality of the building on which they may be expending hundreds of thousands of dollars in professional fees to design and millions of dollars to construct—before the project is completed.

Frequently, institutional administrators and trustees hire architects who are "problem solvers." Sounds impressive. Afterward, those same administrators remark that the consultant team solved the problems, addressed the needs, but ultimately—something was missing. Louis Kahn, one of America's most historically eminent architects, once said, "Need is just so many ba-

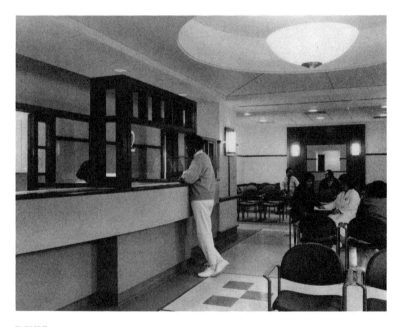

FIGURE 5-4
HOSPITAL OUTPATIENT DEPARTMENT
●*Judicious use of limited funds can provide superior environments.*
Outpatient departments often serve the medically indigent in a community. The architect's challenge here was to provide a dignified, functional, and maintainable physical environment within a very low capital budget. Through the use of plastic laminate, painted gypsum board, and vinyl composition tile enhanced by selected wood detailing and special lighting, this hospital-based clinic experienced an increase in its projected annual visits from 90,000 to 120,000 after its first year in new quarters. We would like to believe the physical environment contributed something to this success. Photo courtesy of Norman Rosenfeld, FAIA Architects.

nanas." What separates "building" from great architecture is the ability to encapsulate desire. Great architecture expresses the aspirations of an institution, while it solves basic needs. The architectural design process should reveal windows of opportunity not previously contemplated and thereby provide solutions that will enhance operations in an uplifting environment. We call this approach "value added" services—but a building should also motivate and inspire the people within. This is particularly relevant to institutional projects where the complexity of space needs, functional adjacencies, technological imperative, and regulatory constraints provide an often nightmarish challenge even to the best of architects. But succeed they do! [Norman Rosenfeld is one who succeeds often in creating beautiful buildings for this client type. Some examples of his projects are given in Figures 5-2, 5-3, and 5-4.]

Patience Is a Virtue

Within a given institution, there are opportunities for a diversity of architectural projects—from low-end maintenance to high-end design of new buildings. Politically astute architects such as Cathy Simon, FAIA (who writes, in the following contribution, about a prestigious private school), know how to establish and maintain excellent working relationships with clients. These relationships support the provision of high quality service and further enhance the likelihood that the architect will be considered for the institution's next project.

Cathy J. Simon is the Director of Architecture and one of five founding principals of Simon Martin-Vegue Winkelstein Moris (SMWM). Under Ms. Simon's leadership, the San Francisco architecture, interior design, and planning firm has established itself locally and nationally with an expertise in institutional, educational, and civic design projects. Ms. Simon, President of the Harvard Graduate School of Design Alumni Council, is currently a Distinguished Visiting Professor at the University of California at Berkeley.

In 1989, my firm (SMWM) was contacted by Lick-Wilmerding High School, one of San Francisco's premier educational institutions, to present our qualifications for a range of architectural services. Two projects were in the offing: The first was utilitarian in the extreme; the second was so attractive as to render the first a necessary evil. After a successful interview process,

SMWM entered into an intriguing evolution of architect–client relations that has resulted in four years of steady improvement for the School. The intrigue lies in the journey traveled between the first and second project.

Contrary to my hopes of an expansive first project, our work with Lick-Wilmerding began with a mundane series of quick fixes. Twenty years earlier a freeway, I-280, had been cut through the southern part of the city, along the school's eastern property line. Finally, after years of intrusive traffic disruption, funds for noise abatement had been made available through CALTRANS, California's mega-agency that controls transportation infrastructure. CALTRANS had performed an acoustical study and had developed a cost-driven strategy that suggested sealing all the operable windows in the school and providing mechanical ventilation, but no new ceilings, no new lighting, no new finishes.

Lick-Wilmerding's Board of Trustees considered the noise abatement projects to be the School's highest priority. The second and, in the Board's view, slightly peripheral task involved preparing a master plan for future development of the School. When Lick-Wilmerding first contacted us, they informed us of both tasks (in that order). As design-oriented architects, we found it difficult to embrace the challenges afforded by the narrowly defined noise abatement project, but the prospect of designing a master plan for a wonderful school on a large, open urban site was utterly irresistible. We also knew that the potential of the master plan project was evident to Al Adams, the visionary headmaster of Lick-Wilmerding and the driving force behind the project, and to David Plant, a brilliant, service-oriented builder and alumnus of the school. There is no doubt that we were hired in part for our experience with the State of California, but principally because we were inspired by the opportunity to create a place for learning that matched the extraordinary goals of the school.

We enthusiastically embarked on the immediate tasks, interacting with CALTRANS on the one hand, and the school administration and faculty on the other. True to our profession, we attacked the pragmatic and mundane physical needs of the School, and at the same time began to establish a physical development path for it. For the former, we relied on CALTRANS' acoustical study of environmental noise; for the latter, we solicited information from the administration and teachers in an open-ended collaborative process. As we jumped through bureaucratic hoops and calculated cubic feet of air per minute and noise reduction coefficients, we also speculated about the future shape of the School, marrying philosophy with physical design. As architects of this vision, we viewed the shortcomings of the School as opportunities to redefine the campus image and create a sense of place where previously none had existed.

Part of the CALTRANS work involved evaluating existing facilities: Seismicity, deferred maintenance, environmental quality, visual characteristics, and use of space. For example, our condition assessment revealed that one of the School's four principal structures, a wood frame industrial building housing wood, metal, and machine shops and the drafting studio, was "seismically nonexistent." We therefore optimistically proposed replacing it with a new shop building on an adjacent site, to help define the campus edges while allowing ongoing programs to continue during construction. In place of the existing shop building, we proposed a new library/student center to provide a physical and metaphorical, intellectual, and social link between the technical and liberal arts on the campus.

The reaction to our proposal was unexpected. While appreciating the thinking and work that had informed our suggestions, the Board of Trustees did not readily accept the scope of change that we envisioned. During the process, they had little opportunity to interact with us, and therefore did not "own" the proposal. Rather than support our concept to replace the shop building that summer, they hastily agreed to upgrade the existing shop building, paying for the work out of the endowment funds, and therefore tacitly agreeing to keep the structure for a long time. (Independent schools, in my experience, are loathe to spend money on temporary improvements.) The following summer, the CALTRANS noise abatement proceeded concurrently with seismic, life safety, and handicapped access remediation of the existing classroom building.

Ironically, these pragmatic projects—seismic upgrades triggered by the existing facilities assessment, funds for noise abatement becoming available through CALTRANS, and the presence of a handicapped student who needed to be accommodated—were a catalyst for renewed thinking on the part of both the Board and Administration. The moment had arrived to address profound and complex needs for the school. These were several: The inadequacy of student seating and the collection space in the library, the lack of a student center, a misplaced student cafeteria, cramped quarters for both general classrooms and the visual and performing arts, little flexibility in room sizes to enable the emerging variety of teaching styles, poor acoustical adjacencies (math classes next to instrumental music classes), and dysfunctional intellectual adjacencies (foreign language departmental offices next to shops).

Thus in 1993, four years and several projects later, having learned from the previous experience, we embarked on a master plan study. This time, we created a methodology that involved full participation of the Board, faculty, administration, and students. The process was intriguing, synthetic, iterative, and rewarding. Interestingly, the students, all of whom are required to study architecture as freshmen, were some of the most acute, intelligent, insightful, and outspoken clients I have known. The master plan, which will be implemented over time, allows for flexible phasing and integration of emerging technologies. It envisions a new image for the School that builds on the tradition of the comfortable and unassuming existing buildings that characterize the Lick-Wilmerding present campus.

The proposed design is in every way a physical manifestation of the school's mission, purpose, and curriculum. Lick-Wilmerding's educational program is based on its dictum, "Head, Heart, Hands." (Head: The education of the mind. Heart: The nurturing of a social conscience. Hands: The training of applied skills.) For example, our master plan specified the use of exposed structure and assembled industrial skin, as a continued reflection of the hands-on teaching at the center of the school's curriculum. To accommodate the three-tiered structure of the Lick-Wilmerding program, we included in the master plan a variety of settings from large lecture rooms to small group study/conference spaces in which the rich and diverse education proposed by the School can generously take place. The plan recognizes the validity of the departmental identities while making numerous explicit and implicit connections among disciplines.

Interestingly, it took the existing facilities assessment and the various practical remodeling steps to realize this new vision. For the School and the architect as well, the process unfolded with a life of its own; now it has assumed the conventional fundraising-implementation rhythm so familiar in independent institutional contexts. We expect our relationship with Lick-Wilmerd-

FIGURE 5-5

The master plan of Lick-Wilmerding High School in San Francisco, showing existing buildings and proposed construction. Bottom plan is first level; top plan is upper level. Drawings courtesy of SMWM.

FIGURE 5-6
Model photos reveal the three-dimensional expression of the proposed master plan. Bottom is an aerial view looking west; top is an eye-level view of the new cafeteria in the foreground with studios and library beyond. Photos by Gerald Ratto Photography courtesy of SMWM.

ing to be very rewarding and very long. We hope that realizing the master plan will result in an educational environment as inventive and multivalent as the students, faculty, and administration at the School.

CHAPTER 6

THE POLITICS OF DESIGN: RACE AND GENDER

Race and gender appear to be increasingly appreciated as mediators of the relationship between architects and clients. The
contributors to this chapter are extraordinary pioneers in architecture's effort to shed light on some very uncomfortable but
crucially important issues.

While exploring and analyzing the specific problems posed by
certain kinds of discriminatory patterns, there is the added benefit of simultaneously achieving a fuller understanding of how
bureaucracies behave in the most general sense. In the following
material, Jack Travis poignantly states, "The biggest disadvantage [to being black or female] is that the captains of industry,
the people who are in the power positions, are white males who
give work to architects who are in a traditionally white male
dominated profession. So all of us have to fight."

A Black Architect on a Mission

Jack Travis is a black architect on a mission.
    *It was early spring when I visited Jack in his office on West 29th
Street in Manhattan. A friendly and frenzied staff, curvilinear perfo-
rated sheet metal partitions, exposed concrete block, and African furnishings signaled a workplace that was busy, with a unique design
flair.*

Jack Travis' book, African American Architects in Current Practice *(Princeton Architectural Press, New York, 1991) was reviewed in* Progressive Architecture *in March, 1993. I was quite intrigued with the review, and subsequently the impressive quality and message of the book itself. It is the first book to promote the identity and work of black architects practicing today.*

I wanted to learn more about the meaning of "mainstream practice" from Jack's perspective, and how he concurrently maintains a strong cultural identity. I asked him for an interesting architect–client story, and, more generally, what motivates his practice, writing, and teaching.

What especially struck me about our conversation was his characterization of the specific and very personal nature of the relationship between architect and client. Travis highlighted the frequent struggles for control and the challenges to communication as independent of the more globally important themes involving race and ethnicity in America today. In the instance presented here, the politics of architect–client relations is as crucial a factor in a successful outcome as is attention from both architect and client to the politics of race relations and achievement of social and cultural parity.

The following story from my conversation with Jack Travis revolves around his design of the renovation of filmmaker Spike Lee's home in Brooklyn, New York.

A Brownstone Grows in Brooklyn

AP: Can you tell me how you met Spike, and how he subsequently selected you as the architect to design his new home?

JT: The day I met Spike Lee, on that Monday, I was sitting for two hours because they were already doing the first readings for the movie *Jungle Fever.* Then Spike came down, he walked past me once or twice, and didn't know who I was. Then he asked Wesley Snipes [the star of the movie], "Where's the architect, man?"

"He's right there, fool!"

"Man, I'm sorry. I didn't know who you were." Then I looked at Spike. Here was this man who had three calls waiting—one from Warner Brothers for the movie *Malcolm X,* another from the Teamsters for a quarter of a million dollars on equipment to use in the street scenes for *Jungle Fever,* and I can't remember the other. And this man was talking to me! Hold—on those other phone calls!

Spike had on open Nikes, he was short, he had the ugliest knees I'd ever seen in life, and I thought this is a CEO from a major company doing high-quality work, dressing the way he wants to dress, and running his business. As long as you can produce and deliver, you can be yourself.

AP: How did your relationship start?

JT: It all started when Wynn Thomas, Spike's set designer, discovered an article illustrating one of my projects: It was the Georgio Armani Boutique—the Emporium Boutique—on Fifth Avenue and 16th Street in New York City, and was featured in the September 1989 issue of *Interior Design*.

Wesley and Spike had been collaborating on this new movie at the time, *Jungle Fever*. Wesley asked Spike if he could get an architect with whom he could mentor, because Wesley did not know any black architects and he wanted to make the part believable to young, black architects. Spike then asked Wynn Thomas to find someone, and Wynn then called us.

At first Wynn suggested that they film part of the movie in my office—and I said, "Fine!" So he came to my office; it was another office—not this one—and he said, "Nooo, I don't think so, this is not quite what we had in mind. But maybe you could work with Wesley."

Wesley came over one evening. We hit it off immediately. Within a week, I was called out to Brooklyn to *Forty Acres and a Mule Film Works, Inc.* to meet Spike. All the actors and actresses were present, and, of course, I was blown away—it was incredible! When I returned to my office, I had a message on my machine from Spike, and it said, "Jack, I need a black architect. Come over to see my house." So I went back to Brooklyn to see Spike's newly purchased brownstone. I sent him a proposal for services and he said it was fine, and I knew he never even read it. He said, "Just do it. We can have this done in a month, right?"

"In a month?"

"Yea, gotta move-in!"

I said, "*Sure,* we can have it done in a month—I don't know exactly *what* will be done in a month, but we can do it." When I tried to explain to him exactly what it entailed, he said, "Oh, how long?"

"Well..."

"How long?" he insisted.

"Probably take a year."

Spike paused and said, "Alright, when can you get started?" Just like that. So I knew from that point on, he'd be a very easy person to work with. All of my staff working on this project were black, and one was Puerto Rican—it was a good team including Vincent Nealy, Adegboyega Adefope, and Buster Tiangco. Spike was very positive.

The Design

AP: In your initial meetings with Spike, did he tell you exactly what he wanted, give you a program?

JT: The first thing Spike said to us was, "I want you guys to respect the house." It was a circa 1868 High Victorian era brownstone. It's probably one of the top three or four brownstones on Washington Park in Fort Green, Brooklyn—and all of them are fairly magnificent—but his was really wonderful. To me it seemed that he was not sure how to make the transition from the existing detail to the kinds of imagery that he wanted for the spaces. So we were supposed to be the mediators to make that change.

Our approach was to come up with a concept and a direction. The relationships of the rooms [to each other] were of course already set. So we thought we would go in and bombard Spike with a great deal of information and show him what we wanted to do—WRONG! We went in there wearing suits and everything; we were going to intimidate this guy—WRONG! He looked at what we wanted to do and said, "I like that, you can do that, don't do this, I'm not listening to that, but this is okay, I don't care about that." He just snapped his fingers—within minutes—he knew what he wanted.

AP: How did you respond to such an opinionated reaction?

JT: We needed to regroup. We went back in and said, "Spike, this is High Victorian," and we wanted to show him what the traditional style was, and he said, "No!" We replied, "Good! Now just let us kind of hang loose and go with the flow."

He loved our next presentation. We just loosened things up; we did not design the spaces fully. Rather, we allowed him to come in with certain imagery and ideas—mostly art—what he thought he should live with including pieces that would be compatible to the transition from the existing envelope to the new imagery. It was a marriage after that—a full go-ahead—that was about four months into the project.

FIGURE 6-1
Front elevation view of Spike Lee's renovated brownstone in Brooklyn by the New York City firm, Jack Travis, Architect. Drawing courtesy of Jack Travis.

The Contractor

AP: Did the process continue smoothly through bidding and construction administration phases?

JT: Drawings were completed about six months into the project. They went out to bid and Spike asked, "Who are these drawings going to?"

I said, "I've worked for five years with Georgio Armani with Herbert Construction as the contractor. They're a very good firm, they'll do the job, and I can beat-up on them if I have to in case there are mistakes or if there are cost overruns, or problems like that."

Spike inquired, "Black owned?"

"No."

Spike repeated: "Black owned."

I said, "I don't know any black contractors in New York City that could do this level of work at this point in time"— which is a ludicrous statement—although it was true. I just did not know anyone; it was ludicrous on my own part, and this is New York City where there are the biggest black talent markets in the country, and still we didn't know anybody. And that pretty much says where African-Americans are: I thought we have to do something about that, and Spike was absolutely right. So we went out looking. Then I went back to him and said, "I found a couple of people but they can't show me any work of this level. Quite frankly, I'm concerned about that because this is my first job with you; I want to work with you and I want this job to be the best that it can be."

"Well I want black contractors."

I said, "Let me tell you about Herbert Construction. They do have a black person on the executive committee, he's a good friend of mine. He's the estimator."

Spike responded: "*One?* Out of how many?"

"Seventy."

"No. Un uh. Un uh. I don't want that. If they're going to be working on my house, they're all going to be black owned firms, including the subcontractors. Go out and find them."

So we went out and now we have a list of all these black contractors and subcontractors, which is really wonderful. But when it came to marble and plaster work—there are no African-Americans in this work. Spike understands that and then it's, "Okay get the best."

AP: The next step was selecting the general contractor?

JT: We ended up using a friend of his as the general contractor who had done some work for him before, and without drawings. The work, in my opinion, was not great but I had faith in these people after speaking to them that I could talk to them and communicate the kind of quality that I wanted. Of course, this would be very good for them because it would be their biggest job to date and again *it was what Spike's philosophy was all about: Helping black owners catapult to the next level of professional accomplishment.*

The Need for Better Communication

AP: As the project was nearing completion, did any conflicts arise between you and Spike?

JT: We had only one major argument with Spike: It was about the move-in date. He chose a date that was inopportune for us; and we had given him three dates before that on which he had agreed to move—and did not tell us otherwise. We had no chance to regroup. I had another project going, I had to be out of town on the weekend he decided to move in, and he gave us only a couple of days prior warning. It was disastrous. There are always those little things that never come together but ideally *can* come together with a little bit of supervision and coordination. Because I wasn't there initially, there were workers coming in and out for two or three months—decisions were made by Spike to do things that should have been made by Spike *with* me. Things like furniture: There were some fairly large items that needed to be coordinated and it could have ended much better.

The lines of communication simply broke down. If I had been able to be there—if he had moved in on one of those agreed-to dates—or if I could have cancelled my plans when he did move, it would have ended better. I think we could have made a list together, and I could have explained to him why things are the way they are and I could have then given him a schedule, and of course held to that schedule. With other business commitments, I was never able to connect with him and get the schedule down.

AP: Was he inaccessible to you because of his celebrity status?

JT: Absolutely. He had final editing, distribution, and publicity to deal with on *Jungle Fever*. Then *Malcolm X* was gearing-up big time. It was going to be the biggest thing of his career, and he was just not available. The house was not a major part of his agenda at that time. In his mind, it was very important, but he never understood the full scope of work until very late in the process.

Spike had a *ton* of stuff! He was living in one garden apartment about six doors down from the new place and we thought, okay, he's moving into five stories now, how much could he have? Immediately, when he moved in, the plan was obsolete. The man had 36 pairs of glasses, over 200 pairs of sweats, and 100 pairs of sneakers. How is he going to get married and raise a family in here?

AP: You were surprised!

JT: We should have tried to elicit all this much earlier in the process. I have learned my lesson. Now we stop and take a detailed look at inventory. We set up a clear, detailed schedule and if clients are not available, then we add time to the schedule, and that has to ultimately add fee. Spike put up with us too. There were things we did not coordinate and things we could have done better. I think our drawings were three weeks late. I was editing my book at that time. He was very nice about it. We asked for payments at the most inopportune times for him and there was no more than a word and he found a way to get them to us. When I gave him the biggest invoice, which was when the construction drawings were done, and he hadn't seen them at that point, a *big* invoice, he looked at it and said, "If I pay you tomorrow, is that okay?"

AP: Spike seems like a remarkable and even an eccentric individual.

JT: When I hear people say, "He's a racist, isn't he?," my response is that you're reading white media coverage. If you look at what happens in *Ebony* or *Jet* about this man, does it say that he's a racist? You're reading *The New York Times* or listening to network news—if you listen to *Tony Brown's Journal*, if you listen to *BET News*—black people know what this man is trying to do. There's no other black entrepreneur doing it to his level.

Now we're doing other projects for Spike including show-room space for his record and fashion companies, and we have some inner-city kids involved, kids who are from troubled, disadvantaged families—who are going to help us do the interior work. We've set aside some areas for them to work on.

On Black Architects Today

AP: Who has had great influence on your career in architecture?

JT: Spike, my mother, and Rushia Fellows are my wake-up call. Rushia Fellows was the first black architect that I ever met. I was in third-year architecture school before I met my first black architect—able to do all the things my white counterparts could do. How can that be? It hit me like a ton of bricks.

AP: What can you say about the advantages and disadvantages of being an African-American architect, and does race enter into the politics of architect–client interaction?

JT: I don't know if there are any advantages to being black in the profession of architecture today. Architecture is still so white male dominated. I equate the profession of architecture to the professions in general—like the sport of golf is to sports in general. White people play golf. I think that white men do architecture now, although it's changing, more so for women, in the schools.

The biggest disadvantage is that the captains of industry, the people who are in power positions, are white males who give work to architects who are in a traditionally white male dominated profession. So all of us have to fight. It is very tough to fight because there is a network, there is a subconscious network set-up where white men just seem to relate, get along better with other white men, and they take it for granted that this is the way things should be. And when a person of color or a female comes into it, many of them are kind of surprised, not prejudiced, but really uncomfortable. Then there are people who are outright prejudiced and then there are just a very few people who will give it a go. I'm talking about the people who are the problem—and there are a few of them but they happen to be in the very powerful positions. It's difficult to get to these people. Then once a person comes in, he or she is representative of her whole gender or race. So if you screw-up, even a little bit, or if you make them uncomfortable, that's it. They're not going to try again. They go back to white men, and even if the white men screw-up, they're at least comfortable.

AP: What's really shocking to me is the number of black architects—what is it—1 percent? How can we address the problem?

JT: African-Americans represent less than 1 percent of all architects practicing today. There should be 12 times as many black architects. Blacks are 13 percent of the country—twenty-nine million blacks in America—the second largest population of Africans outside of Africa.

What I'm challenged by most is the architectural curriculum in the schools, and the way students are taught. There are a lot of issues that are not being addressed, particularly the urban context and interior design—which is how people relate to buildings. Cultural aspects of architecture and the architect's responsibility to society are, for the most part, ignored. Studios should be provided where students have an alternative to explore issues that are socially and culturally based, along with the existing studios that are design or formalist based. The schools have to broaden their whole outlook, where architecture programs energetically promote urban planning, environmental design, landscape architecture, and interior design in the same complex. It's now primarily all about form—and that's not what people really relate to—people relate to the sensual feel of the space, and all five senses play a role.

We need writers, editors, photographers, and so on to come out of the architectural curriculum. We need to have a place for people who are not going to do new buildings, but who are going to talk about how the environment needs to come together and how we can look at the environment in a more positive way.

I lecture frequently in the schools. When I mention Georgio Armani and show slides of my work for him, the white male population listens. When I mention Spike Lee and describe my work for him, the black population listens. You have to be able to touch people on all bases, and then you can hit them with your message!

Politically Incorrect in Wichita

Charles F. McAfee, FAIA, NOMA, is a distinguished black archi-
tect with a gleam in his eye that is apparent even through the tele-
phone lines. Like Jack Travis, McAfee's discussion (below) has the
personal and professional transactions between an architect and a
fine client superimposed upon an enduring and pervasive societal
racism.

While illustrating how a successful project and satisfied client very
much result from genuine connections between individuals, it is also
disturbingly clear that cultural differences and the associated prejudice
can creep into and weaken the best of relationships, and create a
special brand of politics we must strive to recognize and ultimately
avoid.

Mr. McAfee has had an eminent career in architecture. His firm
(Charles F. McAfee, Architects/Planners) is one of four selected to
lead the programming, design, and construction management for the
1996 Olympics in Atlanta. He recently won three design awards
from the Kansas Society of the AIA, he was Past President of the
National Organization of Minority Architects, and he has lectured
nationwide and served on the boards of numerous civic organiza-
tions. McAfee is based in Wichita with branch offices in Dallas, At-
lanta, and Oklahoma City.

One day with a big sky over Wichita, I had a call from Britt
Brown, a client that I had for about three months. We'd dis-
cussed an addition for a new computer center for the Wichita
Eagle and Beacon Publishing Company.

I went to Britt's office as requested with a blank AIA contract
(one of the Standard Forms of Contract between Owner and
Architect). The program had grown to include the business department, library, editorial department, Britt's executive offices,
and complete remodeling to the balance of the third floor. During a conversation that lasted approximately five minutes, he
had penciled-in the blanks for the fee and the retainer, and
called his secretary and instructed her to type the contract and
bring a check for the retainer. I had only been in business for a
short time, and this was my first major client. I thought that
this was the way the process was supposed to proceed.

I designed the addition, and Britt approved everything. He
called his secretary once again and instructed her to send me a
check. We started construction and Britt left Wichita to write
news articles about the war in Vietnam.

We finished the project a couple of weeks before Britt returned. Shortly thereafter, I received a phone call. Same instruc-

tions: Bring a blank contract. I asked Britt, "What are you going to do now?"

He responded, "Just bring the contract."

I arrived at Britt's office; he pushed the controls on his desk to open the drapes and said, "You see those railroad tracks?" (It was a double track that dead-ended at the front property line.) I commented that I had seen those tracks before, and Britt continued, "I bought the tracks and we are going to design a building over them."

As usual he was in a hurry, and I worked all week to design this five-story addition with a full basement to receive and store newsprint, move it to the presses, then back to the second level for processing and delivery. The design was approved in seven days—after a five minute presentation, a check, and instructions to proceed with construction documents. I thought, "Right!"

We started construction soon after and then one day I got this rather emotional call from Britt, "Can you have lunch with me?" When I arrived on time, he had already finished his first scotch and water and had ordered a second. I asked what was wrong. He was furious.

He said that he had been out to his club, the one I could not belong to, and had been asked, "Brown, what do you mean hiring the nigger to do your work?" As I sat there, Brown continued, "I won't mention his name, but he's one of our so-called

FIGURE 6-2
New computer center addition for the Wichita Eagle and Beacon Publishing Company. Photo courtesy of Charles F. McAfee, FAIA, NOMA Architects/Planners.

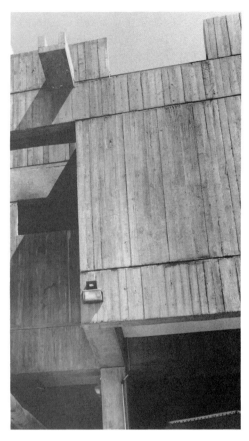

FIGURE 6-3
(Left) View of entry reveals sculptural massing as addition joins the existing building. (Right) Detail of board-formed concrete finish. Photo courtesy of Charles F. McAfee, FAIA, NOMA Architects/Planners.

leaders. My answer to him was, 'First of all the nigger, as you call him, is the best architect in town and second, it's my money.'"

One day I drove to the site to check on the progress of construction. I had parked my car and headed toward the building. Britt's uncle, the Chairman of the Board, came out of the building and was also looking around. He had reached an age of forgetfulness and with this look of bewilderment on his face, asked if I knew where his car was. It was right in his parking space where he had put it. Then he said, "Mr. McAfee, would you mind driving me to my barbershop?" This guileless, almost child-like request led to many subsequent philosophical discussions on education, business, sports, the Kansas history of each other's ancestors, and how our respective families thought about problems confronting the races.

I was jolted back to reality one day as I was reading the morning paper. I saw a page that made me very annoyed. I called Britt to see if he was in and went to his office. I showed him the page on which the only two articles about black people in the newspaper appeared. One article was a story about Dr. Martin Luther King, Jr. receiving the Nobel Peace Prize, and next to that a picture of Sammy Davis, Jr. kissing May Britt.

Later, a very small article full of falsehoods about me appeared in the paper. I was furious. I called and again went to Britt's office. I asked if he had read the article. He said he had not seen it, called the newsroom, and asked the reporter to come to his office. This "journalist" arrived immediately. Britt asked, "Where did you get your information?"

He answered: "A reliable source."

"Did you call Mr. McAfee?"

"No."

"Meet Mr. McAfee."

This episode underscores the importance of addressing and resolving any *political issue as it arises within the architect-client relationship to ensure an ongoing and truly collaborative partnership.*

Gender, Marketing, and a Client's Faith

Carol Ross Barney, FAIA, is a very talented architect, who, through political savvy, is able to create opportunities for her firm. She recounts one such effort and clearly demonstrates that design ability alone is not adequate to establish and maintain a viable practice.

Ms. Ross Barney is President of the Chicago architectural firm, Ross Barney Jankowski, Inc. She recently served as the Chair of the AIA Women in Architecture Committee, and her firm is the recipient of several National AIA Honor Awards.

The Selection

Among the many, sundry, and generally minor subjects that are not covered in architecture school is the nature of clients. Clients, from a student's perspective, are always benevolent and highly principled, and the selection process is fair. By extrapolation, we are taught to expect that our clients will select architects based on their creativeness and ethical purity. Since most architects are attracted to their profession for reasons that include a societal consciousness and rarely include economics, it is not a big surprise that we also run our businesses with a great deal of naiveté.

I started my own firm in 1981, following a mutual parting of the ways with my employer. While I contemplated my future, two of my former clients called to inquire if I would continue working for them. So without any planning, I was in business.

Those first few months were flush. Another client called. Soon four of us were working, just out of my two-story house, and shortly after that, offices in a building I had designed for my previous employer. Unfortunately, after about six months, it seemed that everyone who had ever wanted me as their architect had already called.

In desperation, I began my search for clients, an epic undertaking that continues to dominate my time a dozen years later. I quickly learned some basic rules. Projects do not select architects, people do. Therefore, you need to know people who will build projects, not projects that are going to be built. First, volume counts. There is no way you ever make enough calls or write too many proposals. Second, quantity and not quality is often the deciding factor in architect selection. For example, people are more comfortable with a designer of 50 mediocre buildings rather than 10 great projects. Most people prefer to work with someone they already know. Accordingly, my search for work concentrated on my former clients.

I had worked for the United States Postal Service while I was with other firms, and they built almost constantly. USPS was a natural for me to pursue, I thought.

The Federal Government is mandated to procure all contracts over 25,000 dollars with public announcements. In the case of architect/engineer services, the procuring agency places an advertisement in the federally published *Commerce Business Daily,* advertising the project and the criteria by which the architect will be selected. Interested firms respond by submitting two Standard Forms, SF254 and SF255. In bureaucracies at least, one might avoid the high stakes wine-and-dine circuit of commercial real estate or the campaign contribution chicken dinner sieve of local government work.

And so my quest for postal work began. I sent in SF254 and SF255 and about six weeks later received a two paragraph response thanking me for my interest but explaining that my firm had not been selected. That was okay, I did not expect a direct hit on the first shot. Twelve months and as many SF254/SF255s later, my frustration was growing.

I called the local USPS real estate office. They said that the chair of the slating committee could tell me more. I called each chair. I learned that there were criteria that were not published in the *Commerce Business Daily.* The typical ad was answered by 75 to 100 firms. It was hard for the slating committee to cut the field down to five or so for the interview, therefore they added qualifications to more easily cull the group down. Only firms in or adjacent to the zip code where the project was located were considered. Since all the projects were mostly in Chicago suburban communities, and most architect/engineers were in Chicago's "Loop" central business district, this worked neatly for them.

Other common added criteria were a minimum of five years in business and 25 employees. This one also worked well since 85 percent of architect/engineers employ less than 10 architects. (Two to three architects typically handle a job this size.)

Since the projects were generally within 30 miles of the Loop and under two million dollars, neither one of these list-shortening criteria seemed particularly relevant. My protests were politely considered and I continued to receive the two paragraph rejection letters. I did notice, however, that some of the advertisements stated that preference would be given to firms owned by minorities. When I asked my USPS contacts about the rationale behind the preference, they told me it was necessary because the minority firms were disadvantaged and were generally less than 25 employees and five years old and therefore didn't meet criteria and were almost certainly not located in the suburbs.

The explanation did give me a valuable idea. I inquired if they ever hired women architects and politely pointed out that women-owned firms wouldn't meet the criteria either. When I asked if they could give preference to women-owned firms, my question was kicked up to the regional manager and finally the headquarters.

Not much after that, an advertisement appeared in the *Commerce Business Daily* for a new post office with preference for minority- *and* women-owned firms. I sent in my SF254/255, was slated for an interview, *and* got the commission for a new branch post office in Glendale Heights, Illinois.

The Design
The Glendale Heights facility was pretty typical for suburban branches. The program included a large workroom where the mail is sorted, offices, locker rooms, a service lobby, and a lock box lobby. Our project manager, Fred Gleave, provided a "functional design" plan that established the critical adjacencies.

Glendale Heights is a medium size, blue collar suburb. Developed in the 1960s and 1970s, Glendale Heights doesn't have a traditional downtown or village center. Shopping and fast foods are located at the heavily commercialized intersection of two major arterial streets.

The Postal Service had selected a site about a half-mile from this intersection in an industrial park. At that time, the Postal Service required the architect to present three alternative designs based on the functional design plan. Because the plan was more or less set, the alternatives were reduced to elevation studies of color and materials.

We visited the Glendale site and other recently completed branch facilities including some in industrial parks. The most lasting impression we had of the new buildings was that they were so similar in expression to their office/warehouse neighbors that they were hardly recognizable as public buildings. We discussed our impressions with Fred and he agreed.

So we concentrated our three alternatives on designs that would distinguish the new post office from its surroundings. Our first inclination was to use forms and details that were "governmental," a common 1980s approach, often called postmodern by critics. But since most detail is of pedestrian scale and our site was viewed at 45 mph from an arterial street, this approach was less than ideal. We briefly considered overscaled detail.

Our second attempt also relied on providing more visual interest to the façade than the typical office warehouse. The third design rejected the notion of using familiar detail and form to distinguish the building. The theory was to use the materials already present in the industrial park but to combine them in unexpected ways. Using the existing white and red brick palette of surrounding structures, we created a bold striped façade that enclosed the workroom. The customer lobby was clad in striking blue glazed brick, giving the building a flag-like appearance (see Figure 6-5). The illusion was completed by adding gold chevrons on the parapet that functioned as skylights and scuppers.

When we presented the three schemes to Fred, we thought he would appreciate the third but opt for the first. After our

FIGURE 6-4
The three elevation studies for the Glendale Heights Branch Post Office. Drawings courtesy of Ross Barney Jankowski Inc., Architects.

FIGURE 6-5
*The flag-like Glendale Heights Post Office. Photo by Barry Rustin Photography,
courtesy of Ross Barney Jankowski, Inc., Architects.*

presentation, he asked which we wanted to build. We answered
the flag scheme, and he approved it without hesitation.

Fred's confidence in our solution was to become invaluable
during the development of the design. He stalwartly defended
us to his own colleagues, the USPS operations people, and the
Village of Glendale Heights.

Other team members were invaluable to the completion. The
USPS construction representative, architect Craig Sharp, was
less convinced than Fred, but also a staunch team player. The
general contractor's superintendent, Nick Karas, was as responsible for the quality of the design as anyone by the end of the
project.

As the building neared completion, it began to attract atten-
tion (not surprising since that was the premise of the design).
Most of the attention was very favorable, culminating with a
Presidential Design Award from the National Endowment for
the Arts and an Honor Award from the American Institute of
Architects, which is generally regarded as the most prestigious
American architectural prize.

Happily, Fred got to receive all the awards for the Postal Service. To this day, the higher-ups at the USPS remain mystified by the attention and praise generated for the building.

Lessons to Learn

Shortly after our commission, the Postal Service developed their "Kit of Parts" approach to design, so the days of uniquely designed facilities are, at least temporarily, over. Consequently, we haven't been asked to design another post office. However, we occasionally use our post office "guerrilla style" marketing approach. These tactics aside, the most important element is the trust and confidence of the individual client representatives. This is a rare condition and one that we will always be looking for and trying to inspire.

CHAPTER 7

ALL ABOUT COMMUNICATION

One of the most fundamental elements in making good architecture is *communication* between architect and client through
all phases of a project, from conception to construction. Communication is traditionally defined as "a giving or exchanging
of information by talk, gestures, writing, etc.;" a "close, sympathetic or meaningful relationship." Usually, there is a direct correspondence between quality of dialogue and quality of architecture. This is such a basic truth, yet communicating well is
frankly elusive for many architects.

How can architects facilitate "meaningful" communication?
Certainly clients should bear some of the responsibility as party
to the transaction, but *the architect is the professional,* and therefore it behooves him or her to ensure success. As part of the
architect-selection process, clients should weigh the "chemistry"
factor heavily; if it is nonexistent, then it is likely architect and
client will not be "on the same page," as Mike Ditka would say.

In this chapter, Jeremiah Eck draws an analogy to medicine
and proposes that architects think about clients as if they were
patients to effect better communication; Kirby Lockard believes
that architects owe their clients a "careful explanation of the
intentions and rationale for a building's design;" Bob Greenstreet tells us how to avoid legal squabbles by communicating
well; and stories with happy and sad endings by CRSS Architects and Roger K. Lewis, respectively, begin and end the
chapter.

The Architect and Client Communicating

If They Don't Understand You, You Haven't Said Anything[1]

The firm of CRSS Architects, Inc. (now joined with and operating as HOK) has a long history of providing superb comprehensive serv-

---

1. From *The TIBs of Bill Caudill:* "Last night during a school for instrument pilots sponsored by the Houston Traffic Control Center, FAA, I heard one of the controllers explain the importance of two-way communicators with this astute remark:
IF THEY DON'T UNDERSTAND YOU,
YOU HAVEN'T SAID ANYTHING.
That's the essence of communication."

ices worldwide. On their behalf, Renate Schweiger contributes the following story that exemplifies the ease with which "politics," in the worst sense of that term, may be a direct result of faulty communication between architect and client. The position illustrated here is that power struggle occurs when the principal parties don't understand each other and the only reaction is an escalating defensiveness and a fear that agendas simply cannot be met.

Since its founding in 1946, CRSS has won more than 350 national and international design awards. In 1985, the American Institute of Architects posthumously awarded its Gold Medal to CRSS founder Bill Caudill. The firm pioneered a number of programming and project delivery processes including the intensive on-site work sessions ("squatters") to help clients build consensus among diverse special interest groups.

Every architect has a story of spending time and money producing elaborate plans and models of a building that will never be built. Faced with this possibility due to a severe communication problem, CRSS Architects was lucky enough to get a second chance. What we did with that chance astounded both ourselves and our clients.

We were doing work with an international automobile manufacturer to develop an automotive retail design for a nationwide installation program. Our role was not to design individual dealerships, but to create a prototype that local architects would use. We had a concept we called "branding" that linked design to brand identity through a series of branded elements. Having reached a relatively detailed level of design, it was time to present to the client. The "client" in this case was not one or two individuals, but a group of about 30 people. Within this group there were people from four different countries, speaking three different languages. We were working with foreign clients, and we were having a fairly large communication problem.

We had prepared the traditional architectural presentation. There were plans, sections, elevations, and models. In terms of a typical presentation, we had a lot of good information. The client looked and listened and didn't understand.

A main issue was that we had some sculptural walls in the interior space. The problem was, when we said "walls," the client saw walls in isolation, and the immediate reaction was: "It's going to be claustrophobic. It's going to feel enclosed. The customers won't come in. It's not inviting. We don't want walls!"

The idea was to create a specific customer experience through a sequence of branded elements—as the customer moves from exterior through the interior, these objects build on each other, terminating at the feature product display piece. We were using the walls to define special areas within the larger space. The client could see the objects as "things," but they couldn't see beyond these objects to the experience of the interior space that the sequence of objects created. They became fixated on the walls.

In the first presentation, we were trying communicate the quality of the experience of the interior space more than just the details of the solution—this layout, this material, this finish, this color, and so on. While we knew the principles operating here would work, it was apparent that many in our audience found it hard to match what we were showing and describing to them with their own internal picture of what they wanted. The ideas we were presenting through traditional media did not bring the understanding that we'd hoped for. Instead, the presentation had severely biased the client.

This was a problem because we couldn't begin work on the prototype until we got them to agree on the fundamentals. Because we were working on a prototyping project, it was not typical project delivery. Instead, we were designing a concept that would be rolled out on a national basis. We knew we had a good idea and if they saw it built, if they could "experience" it, they would like it.

The audience made their perceptions very clear. At one point, the Vice President began to talk about a dealership he had seen in Los Angeles: "It was all glass. Beautiful. Everything in the building was glass."

"But look," we said, "that's the way dealerships are now. We are challenging that." But if we couldn't get them to agree to the logic of what we were trying to do, there would never be a prototype built.

They gave us another chance. "We've looked at models; we've looked at drawings; we've looked at perspectives, but we still don't get it." They asked: "What can you do?" In fact, they pleaded with us to find a better way to communicate. All they wanted to see was how they could sell more cars.

Whatever it was we were going to do, they had given us only three weeks to do it. If we didn't solve this communication problem, the project would be over.

Design director Douglas Oliver got the team together: "We know what the client's requirements are. We know that we have the details that fit the requirements. Let's take the viewpoint of

FIGURE 7-1
*(Top) Floor plan and (bottom) front elevation of the automobile dealership
prototype. Drawings courtesy of CRSS Architects, Inc.*

the client and imagine ourselves in their place. Let's try to answer their questions and concerns in a way they can understand.
If we can do that, we will have a project that not only is satisfying to imagine, but also has a chance of becoming an outstanding reality."

We could have removed the walls, put in a lot of glass, and
made some other openings. But, as a team, we decided that what

we had was good. Communication was the real problem for us to solve.

It was the early days of our use of [computerized] visualization, but we decided to take the gamble. "I was skeptical," said Oliver, "that we could actually do it in the three-week time frame." We started with a series of stills and strategized how we could show the build-up of the experience without visualization. Then we created the animation and transferred the animated output to video.

We produced a five-minute video showing the build-up of the concept in an existing dealership. Photorealistic images tracked the sun and changed daytime shadows; the structure was viewed from all directions with texture, reflective surfaces, and multiple light sources; and a walkthrough was created following a typical customer path.

"But as far as the design goes, we didn't change anything," said Oliver. "We literally just recreated the design in visualization."

"This is going to be the thing that puts us over the top," Oliver told the team. "If this doesn't communicate what we are

FIGURE 7-2
Interior detail of customer center of the automobile dealership prototype. Photo courtesy of CRSS Architects, Inc.

trying to do, then there's nothing we can do short of building it. Or starting over."

We began our "last chance" presentation the same way we had done the first presentation by going through the logic using traditional media. When they started the attack, we said: "If you'll hold your questions for a minute, we have one final tool to show you."

We showed the video on a 20-foot screen and two things happened. First, they stood up and applauded. The Executive Vice President of International Operations said, "For the first time in my career, I have completely understood a design presentation." In fact, the same expression was overheard around the room: "Now I understand what you've been saying." Not only had they finally understood the design concept, but they were genuinely excited about the presentation experience.

Second, and more important, is that they decided right there to build two buildings.

"I was dumbfounded," said Oliver. "We had not changed anything on the design." It confirmed what we believed—that the ideas were good, that the client would like them *when they understood them.*

"The thing about visualization," said Oliver, "is what it does for client communication. It's like nothing else I've ever seen." Its real power in terms of communicating a design is that it dispels clients' fears. Most clients can't read drawings; but what's even worse, they think they can. Like the wall in our design, they get fixated on something in isolation and it becomes impossible to alter their perceptions. But doing a "walkthrough" in visualization exposes them to a more complete design experience. By obtaining a higher level of comprehension, the client gets a level of comfort from knowing that what is going to be built is what they understood—no surprises.

In 1973, Bill Caudill spoke about what was then a new design and communications tool that CRSS was attempting to use: Video. "It's a great design tool," he admitted. "But it takes too much expensive equipment. We got back in bed with drawings and models. We were 10 years too soon. I've often wondered, had we stuck to this tool [videotape], how would that have altered our practice?"

Twenty years and many advancements later, video is proving to be one of the most powerful tools for communicating design ideas to all types of audiences. Visualization technology has taken our profession into a brave new world of communication.

By definition, visualization is a form of communication: To form an image that allows us to share with others. And the medium used to share that image is videotape. Utilizing a combination of live video, computer graphics, sound, and animation, the design business is adopting techniques used by the entertainment industry. The by-products of visualization, in this case, the video, gave us a badly needed tool to communicate to our multicultural, multiheaded clients. In the ever-expanding global marketplace, visualization becomes a very effective communication tool that transcends barriers between multicultural teams and clients.

And more to the story. We recently attended the grand opening of one of the two completed dealerships. Everyone who had been at the presentation was there. They were extremely pleased with the results: "All of the things you told us it would do, it does. The things we thought were going to be problems are not." Through the dynamic, realistic imagery of the presentation media, the clients' understanding of the design was so complete that, upon seeing the built product, their comment was: "We've already seen this."

For us, it was a breakthrough in communicating a very complex concept to what is, in more and more cases, a very diverse client group with very complex problems. Architects like to communicate with drawings. But that is not how most clients perceive. Not everyone can read a blueprint; everyone can watch television. It is very important that we explore ways to go beyond our drawings and look through our clients' eyes at how they will perceive something. Visualization is one of the many emergent technologies that affect the way we work and communicate.

Treating Clients as Patients

Without being at all patronizing, architect Jeremiah Eck invokes a clinical metaphor in doing architecture, and proposes that this approach has a profound influence on the politics of the architect–client relationship. He suggests that there is less of a power struggle if the architect thinks of him or herself as a clinician.

In a recent issue of Contract Design, *Editor-in-Chief Roger Yee extended the metaphor: "A lesson we might draw from [a failure in] the doctor's office is that taking time to communicate with the client represents a highly visible and symbolic show of concern that also happens to be quite useful. Shouldn't it be obvious that showing more interest in the client's needs convinces the client of his importance to us—just as knowing more about the client's needs helps us solve them better? We should take the time to listen."*

Jeremiah Eck is Lecturer in the Department of Architecture at the Harvard University Graduate School of Design, Faculty Director of the Career Discovery Program at the GSD, and a practicing architect in Boston, MA. His residential works have won numerous awards and have been featured in over 40 national and international publications including Architectural Record, Architecture and Urbanism, Fine Homebuilding, The Christian Science Monitor, *and* The Boston Globe.

It has become increasingly clear to me over the last few years of practice that architectural clients are in many ways similar to medical patients. Or perhaps put a better way, that architects might regard their clients more as patients who come to them with a health threatening problem that requires a solution.

How many of us actually think of a problem to be solved when we first procure a commission? Or rather, do we think of an opportunity to use the financial capacity or program of a client to create or satisfy our own architectural fantasies? I'm convinced that if we instead think of a client as a patient with a specific problem, that we are more likely to produce a good building and that the desired concomitant result—a beautiful building—will also quite naturally follow.

This approach has other implications since treating or understanding a client as a patient is not always easy. I'm a strong believer in the theory that good clients make good architecture. But what is a good client? Unfortunately, they can be both easy or difficult to work with. Some clients may have only a cold but a rotten disposition; others may have pneumonia and a good disposition. I've had my share of both. To underscore my point, one of my most difficult clients produced one of my best, award-winning projects.

Their project was a very small house; the fee had to be fixed and they had already "fired" two previous architects (which I didn't discover until after the project was complete). But the site was extraordinarily beautiful and on an island; and at the same time, it seemed to me to be just the right kind of project to fill-out my built project-types. In other words, I love doing small houses and this one seemed like a special opportunity. One could easily say I had already made a number of classic errors— at least from a business point of view—but that's a discussion for another story.

From the start they were very difficult, demanding innumerable options. I vividly remember sitting across the dining table, usually at night, discussing the house with them and thinking to myself, "How can they be so demanding—and frankly, so cheap?" I struggled with them both and their needs. It was a marathon that I can honestly say I almost didn't finish. But then one day in the office—I can remember it clearly—the design fell into place. Their problem had been solved, their difficult needs had been satisfied. I'm sure you've all had similar experiences. Of course the relationship and the problem solving were hardly over. Each construction detail was analyzed and put to the "what if" test. And later when the bid documents came out, the contractor was asked to lower his price too.

Though somewhat counterprofessional, that contractor and I held a mutual respect for each other's tolerance of our shared client. Then three-quarters of the way through construction, the hitherto low-budget clients "found" some additional money for some of their last minute additional needs. No money was available, of course, for any additional fees for either the architect or contractor.

When it was all over, the house was extraordinarily simple and elegant, and it won a number of awards for me. All of the Sisyphean efforts had, in some ways, paid off. I've had easier clients since then and more award-winning houses, so I've often asked myself why that one was so difficult. The truth is that I've never really been able to answer the question. Just the particular mix I guess. As I mentioned earlier, I did learn subsequently that there had been two other architects before me. So was I totally off the mark? I doubt it!

The lesson to learn perhaps is that a good client is not just an easy client, but one that brings the best out in us to perform our service as problem solvers. Each client—or patient—has their own particular needs and point of view, and some are more or less difficult than others. Each of us as architects remains the same, tempered by our experiences. So it is really up to us to adjust our services accordingly. Indeed, one of the most difficult aspects of practicing architecture is the need to reinvent the

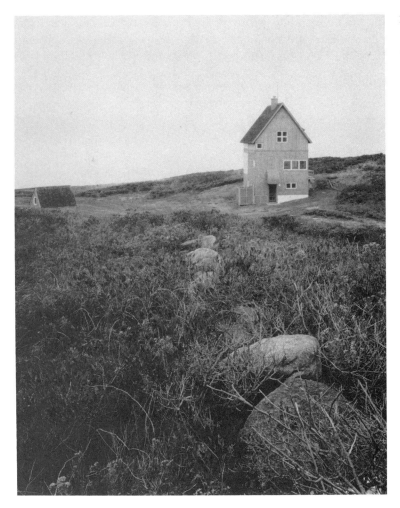

wheel each time for each new client. Why can't they just let us do our jobs as we have learned to do over many years of practice?

The answer of course is that each client has a fundamental right to ask you to solve a problem first, a problem and process that they have never been through before. Like a patient with a doctor, if the health problem is not diagnosed and solved correctly, the doctor has not done his or her job. Thinking of the architectural process in this *clinical* fashion has allowed me to profoundly temper my relationship with most clients. In many ways, our common goal is achieved through a process struggle not a power struggle. If, like a doctor, we begin to think of clients as patients, we may begin to overlook their particular personalities and our idiosyncratic needs, and begin to produce responsive and beautiful buildings again.

Architects as Great Communicators

William Kirby Lockard, FAIA, reiterates below the need for architects to understand how to communicate effectively with clients (and constructors) as basic to providing professional services. He calls for distinct phases of communication that should ideally correspond to phases of the design and construction process.

Professor Lockard has taught for 30 years at the University of Arizona, and has his own practice in Tucson. His books, including Design Drawing, *are classics in the field.*

One of my most satisfying experiences in communicating with clients came while taking a group of my design students on a field trip to a church I had designed some 15 years earlier. We were met by the young pastor, who had come to serve the church five years or so after it was built. He asked if it would be all right with me if he showed my students around the church. I was amazed to hear him explain the building, especially the sanctuary and the way it reflects the Lutheran liturgy, in almost exactly the way I had explained it to the original pastor, building committee, and congregation 15 years ago, using many of the same phrases and analogies.

I have since come to believe that such a verbal explanation of the intentions and rationale for a building's design are a very important part of any architect's professional service. We owe our clients that careful explanation. I even believe the explanation should be an integral part of the cover sheets of our construction documents, so that all those who help build the building have a better understanding of the design's intentions.

We have been slow to realize that architect–client communication is absolutely crucial to the success of any architect, any building project, and, altogether, to the success of our profession as a whole. Our greatest architects have always been great communicators and spent an enormous amount of energy in their effort to understand and be understood. Frank Lloyd Wright's voluminous correspondence and his ability to charm and persuade clients, even when his purposes were questionable, remain truly impressive.

Three years ago, at the University of Arizona where I teach, we initiated a graduate concentration in Design Communication and, having taught the graduate seminar in that concentration and helped several graduate students in their research projects, I have come to two interesting conclusions.

My first conclusion is that, aside from the rich and extensive anecdotal literature about the communications between architects and their clients, there is almost no research on the subject. And further, we are finding that many of the traditional and most strongly held opinions that architects have about communicating with clients are not supported by research. They are just flat wrong. We have found, for instance, that clients are much less impressed and persuaded by elaborate drawings than most architects suppose. Architects have continued to make those beautiful drawings for one another, as a kind of ritual, without ever bothering to find out if they were efficient communications.

Another interesting result of one graduate student's research concerns the ethics of client communication. In extensive interviews with individual members of public client–architect selection committees, one of our Masters students found that architects' "free" sketches, presented at job interviews were almost never perceived as unethical or inappropriate, but simply as a convincing indication of interest in the project.

The second realization that is unmistakably indicated is that, just as we have a lot to learn about successful communication, if we take our understanding of it seriously, we will have a great deal to contribute to communication theory. This potential theoretical contribution is based on the uniquely complex and changing way we must communicate during the process of the design and construction of a building. The context changes from the tentative, questioning, listening communication of programming through the explanation of schematic alternatives to the dialogue of change and refinement to the confident, convincing, persuasive communications that seek approval of the final design; and the media changes just as drastically, from verbal and numerical expressions of needs to two-dimensional conceptual diagrams to complex three-dimensional drawings and models, to intricately detailed construction documents and, finally, to the design intentions that communicate in the masonry, steel, and concrete of the finished building.

We need to be masters of communication and it is time we realized that communication, considered broadly, is perhaps our most essential professional skill.

Legal Pitfalls of Poor Communication

Robert C. Greenstreet, Ph.D., is an expert on legal aspects of professional practice, and has written the following cogent essay regarding the architect–client relationship. He is Dean of the School of Architecture and Urban Planning at the University of Wisconsin–Milwaukee, and has co-authored The Architect's Guide to Law and Practice. *Dean Greenstreet is also a frequent contributor to* Progressive Architecture.

While the architect–client relationship can be viewed from any number of perspectives, one that is perhaps given too little attention is the legal bond that ties the two parties together. This is not surprising given the less than stimulating content of most contractual arrangements, but it is a factor that is ignored at the peril of both parties, as recent statistical reviews show. During the 1980s, legal action against architects reached an all-time high, with 43 percent of insured architects reporting a claim against them in the year of 1984. This alarming statistic did not include noninsured architects or those who settled prior to the claim reaching the insurer's ears. Of these many legal suits, over half of them were brought by clients against their architects and, while the overall number of annual suits against insured architects has dropped to 27.2 percent in 1993, there is still a high proportion of legal action generated during the architect–client relationship.

Why do so many relationships, presumably originally founded on trust and faith, deteriorate into legal squabbles? An extensive review of decided cases including clients and their architects suggests that poor communication, particularly during programming and the estimation of projected costs, lie at the heart of many disputes. The Farnsworth House, for example, is a world renown icon of modern architecture and yet was the catalyst for a nasty fight between Mies Van der Rohe and Dr. Edith Farnsworth. He sued for mechanics lien foreclosure on the architectural masterpiece to recover $28,000 in unpaid fees, while she countersued for $33,000, the exact amount she claimed Mies exceeded his original estimate. Too much focus on the *product* of the relationship, the building, and not enough focus on the *process* of getting it built—which includes constant client updating and involvement on all issues—lead to such problems.

Strong and successful architect–client relationships where legal action is minimized seem to be rooted in solid, well-constructed agreements in which the rights and responsibilities of each side are clearly understood and a "meeting of the minds" has been reached. With clients inexperienced in construction matters, the onus is upon the architect to take the lead in "educating" the client as to the contractual process and the building process that will be necessary in bringing a building project to successful fruition. This is not a patronizing task, but one where the importance of owner participation in decision making and dealing with unexpected change is emphasized so that the client is a deliberate participant in the process. In this way, the client is likely to experience fewer nasty surprises—budget extras, time delays, and so on—or at least be prepared for them and therefore less prone to immediately blame the architect for issues beyond his or her control.

How can this state of grace, a meeting of the minds, be best achieved? Standard Forms of Contract, while an anathema to many attorneys and derided as inflexible or insufficiently advantageous to the client, have the distinct advantage of containing articles and language that are generally understood throughout the construction industry. American Institute of Architects Standard Forms, for example, have been modified through as many as 13 editions by groups representing architects, clients, contractors, and consultants, and offer a relatively level playing field, complete with rules of the game, upon which the parties can establish, define, and comprehend their relationships.

Beyond the contractual capacity they offer, Standard Forms, which come in a range of abbreviated or customized variants, can be very useful as a means of education, enabling an architect to walk a potential client through the contents and enlighten them on the process of construction that is ahead. It's a lot less fun than scribbling pictures on the back of a napkin, but does provide a structured education to a client on the role he or she is expected to play in the upcoming adventure.

Of course, the really important aspect of the architect–client relationship is the success of the building itself, its contribution to the built environment, and the satisfaction of its inhabitants. This endeavor can only be enhanced by a successful interaction between the parties based on a sound contractual footing. This reduces the likelihood of legal action against the architect, increases the prospect of a satisfied client, and therefore a happy and well paid architect—while over 75 percent of architects who sue clients for their fees win, the cost in legal fees, reputation, and bother hardly seem to make it worthwhile. Consequently, the success of the architect–client relationship, the cornerstone of the building process, needs to be firmly established on a professional footing where the need or threat for legal action is substantially minimized.

The Mercurial Client

A vivid example of a client failing to communicate—or at least not listening well—is presented by Roger K. Lewis, FAIA. Alas, in some circumstances, going to court (or at least the threat of legal action) is indeed the only option to reconcile opposing viewpoints. (The biography for Roger Lewis appears in "The Hospitable Tunisians" in Chapter 4.)

At our very first meeting, he exclaimed: "I want this project to be one I can someday show with pride to my grandchildren! That's why I want you to be my architects." We architects smiled, admiring and sharing this residential developer's infectious enthusiasm and can-do aspirations after hearing him describe what he sought to accomplish. He was looking for award-winning architecture.

Our client was the prototype of an entrepreneurial, 1970s would-be iconoclast well into middle-age: Mod clothes, open shirt and leather vest, gold chain necklace and copper bracelets, stylishly long and thick, well coiffed hair. He was constantly in motion, full of nervous energy, always talking and gesturing exuberantly, reviewing design ideas and issuing approvals as he cheered on the architects. "These houses must be top quality, great spaces, finest materials, latest amenities."

For many months, we worked diligently together. He and I became friends, visiting each other's homes and meeting each other's families. Sometimes we would meet in the evening at the trendy restaurant where he regularly held court. He began dating one of my secretaries and didn't hesitate to drop by my office without an appointment, both to visit her and to check the progress of his projects. He was a bright and engaging person, a memorable character in a city of bureaucrats and conformity.

I should have known better. We ended up embittered adversaries in court three years later.

I was the plaintiff—he had refused to pay the last portion of the fee that I was owed. His defense was that my firm had failed to perform adequately. Thirty minutes before the trial, both his and my attorneys persuaded him to settle and pay up. That morning at the courthouse, he and I never spoke to each other, never exchanged glances, our connections long ago severed. Surrounded by his entourage of lawyers and witnesses, he purposely stayed out of sight while I, my attorney, and my project manager sat in the courthouse lobby deliberating our strategy and negotiating with his representatives, to whom it became increasingly obvious that their client would probably lose.

The schism had occurred many months earlier, when final plans had been completed and the developer had hired an independent, professional estimator to prepare construction cost estimates. The estimator telephoned and, audibly distressed, asked me to come immediately to his office to meet with him and our client. I knew something was seriously amiss. When I arrived with two of my associates, our client was on the verge of losing control. Sitting mutely, tensely, his lips pursed and his face exuding anger, he exploded into a fit of rage. Shouting and screaming, he condemned me and my staff for designing houses that were too expensive to build. Moreover, amidst the yelling were accusations that I had been neglectful and inattentive, too busy doing work other than his. In his view, I and my office staff had prepared incomplete and inadequate documents lacking sufficient information for estimating and construction. Also included in his ranting and raving were repeated assertions that he hadn't gotten what he was entitled to and had paid for.

Trying to look squarely at him, his face still flushed with anger but the tension beginning to dissipate just a fraction, I told him that I was leaving, that I refused to be subjected to his abusive language and hysterics, and that I would discuss his concerns only in a rational manner when he calmed down. We left immediately knowing that the relationship was forever finished.

What had transpired and led to this confrontation?

We had designed the project exactly as required, not only complying with all of our client's initial requirements and subsequent requests, but also apprising him continually of the economic consequences of every design decision along the way. The cost estimates came as no surprise to us. The surprise was that our client, a professional and presumably experienced builder, was surprised. Since undertaking the project, national and local economic conditions had changed dramatically—interest rates and construction costs had risen and, most important, the real estate market had weakened substantially. Rather than accepting responsibility for his own specifications, approvals, and economic misjudgments, he chose instead to lay blame for his current financial dilemma entirely at the feet of the architects. He had conveniently forgotten all of our advice and warnings month after month about rising costs. And he was unconcerned that we had, in fact, expended far more time perfecting the designs—with his continual involvement—than normally required, certainly more than we were being paid for.

His behavior was symptomatic of someone whose ego and sense of self-righteousness made it difficult, if not impossible, to acknowledge his own shortcomings or fallibility. Having received bad news, he needed to blame someone other than himself. And this was exacerbated by manic-depressive tendencies. I had seen hints of his mood swings, but had never appreciated how potentially volatile he really was.

After getting over the initial shock of our encounter at the estimator's office, I rebutted his indictments in writing, completed the work remaining under our contract, and hoped that he would pay his debts. The experience was so distasteful that I chose not to meet with him again. Indeed, when he later refused to make final payment, I was at first reluctant to sue him, fearing that it might provoke another explosive outburst, or worse. Yet I also felt compelled not to let him intimidate me or my colleagues—I learned that he had abused, both verbally and financially, numerous other architects and engineers whom he had hired previously. In my case, his bullying wouldn't work.

Despite the outcome, I still recall the promises and aspirations expressed at the outset of the relationship. They were just too seductive to resist.

CHAPTER 8

CORPORATE POLITICS

Few things in life are more political than the workplace. Maalox consumption is but one testament to the universality of covert executive agendas. How then can architects identify their real clients in this context, the movers and shakers of corporate America, much less uncover the pressing tasks to be accomplished? In the first part of this chapter, Roger K. Lewis deftly analyzes the nature of the power structure in corporations and how it impacts on the architect.

Gene Kohn of Kohn Pedersen Fox Associates discusses several projects in which sophisticated, intelligent clients who appreciate the value of high-quality design are able to reconcile the seemingly contradictory goals of making money and being socially responsible. Kohn refreshingly credits his clients as the significant driving force shaping their award-winning buildings.

Closing the chapter is Cambridge architect Thomas Bakalars, who describes a comical case of mistaken identity. Sometimes luck (when combined with talent and ability) is more important than politics, relationships, or antacids.

The Power Structure

Roger K. Lewis, FAIA, pens this next piece on how corporate politics influences the architect–client relationship. (The biography for Roger Lewis appears in "The Hospitable Tunisians" in Chapter 4.)

Consider some of my corporate clients: Development companies replete with multiple partners or stockholders, boards of directors, chief executive officers, vice presidents, project managers, construction managers, sales and marketing managers, purchasing agents, accountants and bookkeepers, and, of course, attorneys. To deal effectively with such clients, the architect must get beyond the corporation's organizational chart.

Normally the corporation's designated project manager is the architect's primary point of contact, the person from whom the architect officially receives instructions. But periodic meetings attended by other corporate officials inevitably reveal that, in fact, there exists a complex political structure internal to the corporation. The architect must seek to understand this structure—the power structure—if he is to achieve his architectural objectives. Accordingly, he must pose and extract answers to several crucial questions.

What really is the corporate pecking order? Who is really the boss? Who proactively leads and who passively follows? Who, if anybody, is the innovator, the risk-taker, and the experimenter? Who obstructs? Are there cliques? And most difficult to fathom but always critical: What are the interpersonal relationships among corporate officials—who is competing with whom, who dislikes whom, who is trying to subvert whom?

Ideally, decisions about architectural propositions shouldn't have much to do with corporate politics. One would think that once project goals, sites, programs, and budgets are adopted, corporation officials would unemotionally allow the architect to carry out and execute the project. But this is rarely the case, especially when powerful and persuasive individuals within the corporation choose to exert substantial influence over the design process. This is even more challenging for the architect when a multitude of such interested and potentially competing officials enter into the fray.

The architect may become a mediator, or may be subjected to lobbying, usually in private and off the record, by individual corporate executives anxious to build a direct alliance with the architect. Especially tricky for the architect is receiving conflicting signals, opinions, or instructions. Since an official line of authority and responsibility is normally established, the architect may be placed in an awkward position if someone bypasses the official line with a request that contradicts what someone else requested. When this occurs, the architect must very carefully navigate his course. He must act ethically and not violate contractual obligations but, at the same time, must avoid entanglements in corporate politics.

Of course, beyond figuring out the power structure of a corporate client, there is one other corporate issue on which architects must focus: Who's in charge of "accounts payable?"

Resolving Profit with Social Responsibility

Rarely in architectural life does a figure appear of such charisma as Gene Kohn of Kohn Pedersen Fox Associates in New York. Kohn speaks openly (below) about operationalizing his strongly held ideals on a canvas of huge economic risks and potential rewards.

Bringing Religion to the Client

Consider the buildings that comprise most cities—commercial office towers, hotels, retail complexes, apartment buildings, and light industrial warehouse and manufacturing centers. The common thread that links these building types is *profit*. They are, for the most part, built by commercial developers to generate income. More importantly though, these buildings have shaped and continue to shape our cities. For that very reason, it is the challenge of every architect to approach the process of working with a commercial client/developer with an overriding great sense of responsibility. Our cities and their architecture share a symbiotic relationship fostering progress that is essential to human vitality and survival. In this context, the politics of architect–client relations deserves special scrutiny.

A city's civic quality and sensibility are dependent upon a common understanding of goals shared by the architect, developer, corporate leader, and agencies such as planning and zoning departments. Historically, architectural design for a developer client is an aspect of our profession that has been heavily criticized. The esoteric architectural community, to a great extent (although now changing), has viewed the commercial building as something other than architecture. This, however, could not be farther from the truth. Our challenge as architects is to "bring religion" to the client and to illustrate the impact and contribution a building can have beyond its mere boundaries.

The first major surge in urban American, postwar commercial development occurred in the late 1950s, the 1960s, and early 1970s. Much of what was built lacked a sense of design consciousness. Many of the early developers entered the real estate field from other businesses without being trained or educated relative to the responsibility at hand. Today's commercial clients are more knowledgeable and conscientious than their predecessors, because of lessons learned from the past and the availability of high caliber university programs specializing in real estate development.

What *has not* changed is the ultimate goal of the developer client: Profit. The potential for profitability controls the budget and schedule of the project—it dictates the type and size of the building within the established ordinances, and is influenced by the amount of financing the project will receive. Admittedly, a struggle often exists to achieve architectural quality in the face of budget constraints; outstanding design services are often viewed as expensive and/or unnecessary by some commercial clients. Since the early 1980s though, the "signature" architect-designed building, speculative or otherwise, has become more commonplace. Educated, visionary developers have some notion that "architecture" will ultimately benefit their cause. The names of leading, well-recognized design firms are often used to attract financial institutions for equity participation, and to market the building to prospective tenants. As a result there has been, until the economic downturn of the 1990s, a constant competition among design firms and their developer clients to elevate the level of buildings in today's urban centers—this can be seen as good for all those involved, particularly the city and its citizens.

Gerald Hines, President of Gerald Hines Interests, Houston, and George Klein, Chairman of Park Tower, New York, are excellent examples of "architecturally aware" commercial clients. They consistently use the "signature" firms to design their buildings. In turn, the quality of their buildings allows for higher rents as tenants are willing to pay more to be associated with a building that has a high profile and *engages it surroundings*. Critics cite the "snob appeal," but in actuality it works to benefit all parties involved: The owner, the user, the architect, and the passerby. It forces us and our clients to think critically about what is being designed, where, for whom, and *how it relates to its immediate context,* specifically its neighbors and community.

The Power of Architects' Patience and Clients' Faith
In 1976, senior level executives of the American Broadcasting Companies—New York, who had made the acquaintance of Sheldon Fox and myself several years earlier, selected Kohn Pedersen Fox (for its first commission) to complete a series of master planning studies for their operation located on Manhattan's upper westside. Soon after we completed the New York study, Thomas Klutznick, President, and George Darrel, Vice President, of Urban Investment & Development (now a division of JMB Realty Corporation) contacted us. They had learned that ABC—Chicago was looking for new studio and office space. They asked us to prepare a design proposal for a one million square foot office building that would house at its lower levels a new home for ABC—Chicago.

The site was a unique edge location where the orthogonal city grid met the bend of the Chicago River creating a triangular parcel. We saw it as one with tremendous opportunity, where opposing forces of the rigid urban matrix and of the flowing, curvilinear waterway offered the perfect setting for a bold, significant architectural statement. From a development point of view though, the site was considered to be in a "soft" location—meaning the area immediately surrounding it was underdeveloped and less desirable than others in the Loop.

Tom Klutznick had a great vision of the building he wanted to erect on the site. He was willing to risk the location issue because he was convinced a successful building would generate future development. It would help turn the area around and reconnect it to the city fabric. His commitment to the city of Chicago, concern regarding urbanistic issues, and desire to add to its community were unyielding. Some time passed after we submitted our proposal. ABC was to be the major tenant with office, studio, and technical space located at the lower six levels, one of which was below grade providing easy access to lower Wacker Drive and the environs of Chicago beyond. Ultimately, though, they decided against relocating.

For the following year, a finely crafted, small-scale model of our scheme sat on a shelf in Klutznick's office. He reflected, and increasingly recognized and appreciated the merits of the design,

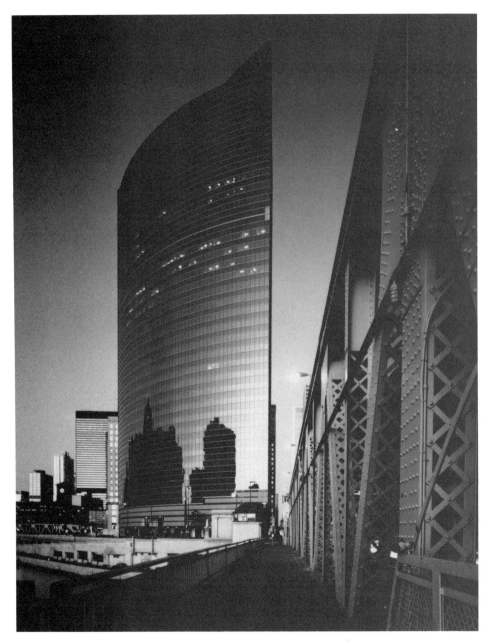

FIGURE 8-1
View of 333 Wacker Drive from across the Chicago River. Photo by Barbara Karant, courtesy of Kohn Pedersen Fox Associates.

knowing that even without ABC, the concept of the proposed building (which he helped to form) held together very well. In 1981, he called to tell us he wanted to go ahead with the project as a speculative venture—and the rest is history. 333 Wacker Drive has in many ways become the definitive example of Chicago's most recent architectural surge. Its symbolic, curvilinear front is highly visible and well-articulated. The building relates to the adjacent Loop surroundings, while majestically asserting itself on the city skyline by reflecting the changing light of day. Its success lies in the strength and simplicity of its form, and is largely responsible for KPF's rapid ascent to architectural notoriety. Klutznick and Darrel were courageous enough to place the utmost of confidence in our young, relatively untested firm. It was one of several successful risks they took. The process and personalities involved proved to be the catalyst for good design. With 333 Wacker Drive as an inspiring force, surrounding sites have been developed, adding to the cohesiveness of Chicago and its urban experience along the river's edge.

Making Profit and Urban Redevelopment Consubstantial
Similarly, our work at One Logan Square deals with challenging site issues and concerned and competent clients. Philadelphia is my home town, and as a result I felt a great sense of responsibility to this project. The site was the last undeveloped parcel on Logan Square, which dates back to William Penn's original master plan of 1683 for Philadelphia. Since the City Beautiful Movement, the Square has served as the institutional node of the city. For 33 years it was a parking lot, and while a number of suggestions, studies, and proposals had been considered, no action was ever taken.

We believed that the difficulty of this project was that this site, which we referred to as "the missing tooth," was very important to Philadelphians for a variety of reasons. Many different interests had to be satisfied due to the rising influence and power of planning, preservation, community, arts, traffic, and political commissions. This was a complex task that required substantial planning and creative thinking; five years worth of earlier proposals for the site by other noteworthy architects were rejected.

In 1979, KPF was approached by PIC/Cigna Insurance, the owners of the site, and asked to complete a proposal within a month; they knew of an established law firm, Morgan Lewis & Bockius, who was aggressively looking to relocate to new office

FIGURE 8-2
Site Plan of Logan Square,
Philadelphia, PA. Drawing
courtesy of Kohn Pedersen
Fox Associates.

space. PIC/Cigna asked for a development with one million square feet of office and hotel space. We worked closely with the city in our planning and design, and in one month we had a scheme that all the involved parties favored. Soon after the lead tenant, Morgan Lewis & Bockius, committed to the building, Urban Investment & Development Co. (of 333 Wacker Drive fame) joined the team and brought with them their commercial urban development expertise. As well, The Four Seasons Hotels Limited was selected to participate in the project and manage the hotel.

In five months, we had received all the necessary approvals from the city agencies involved, and construction began soon thereafter. The end result, a low-rise luxury hotel directly on the square and a high-rise commercial office tower set back 200 feet linked by a large courtyard, is a hybrid expression that completes the square while respecting the historical significance of the immediate surroundings: The square is in the front and the down-

FIGURE 8-3
*View of hotel façade from
Logan Square. Photo by
Norman McGrath,
courtesy of Kohn Pedersen
Fox Associates.*

town business district in the back. The true success of this project is marked by the *teamwork, vision, and cooperation of all the parties involved.* We arrived at a means to achieve an appropriate architectural fit, all the while keeping sight of the client's need to generate profit and the city's desire to retain the classical character of the site. One Logan Square is the only commercial building on the square, yet it is reserved and subdued enough to accord with the harmonious, institutional climate of its setting.

The Value of the Demanding Client
KPF's professional relationship with the Procter & Gamble Company for the design of their new consolidated world headquarters in Cincinnati, Ohio of 1985, best illustrates how well this type of relationship can work. The scope of this project involved adding 800,000 square feet of office space to an existing complex of 600,000 square feet for the consumer products giant. P & G strongly identified with the city of Cincinnati—it had been home to their very conservative, diverse international operation since the founding of the company some 150 years earlier. They were committed to maintaining their low profile and to being sensitive to the culture and traditions of their city.

Their project team started by composing a list of many different firms who they believed were capable of achieving their goals. These firms were presented a questionnaire and, based on their responses, P & G reduced the list to 12 firms. Preliminary interviews were conducted where they discussed each offices' philosophical approach to the project, which narrowed the list to 8 firms who were then interviewed in their respective offices. The P & G project team decided on three final firms to be considered for the commission, all of which were from New York City—SOM, I. M. Pei & Partners, and us, KPF.

We were asked to give our views and ideas relative to a master plan adopted a year earlier by the P & G expansion committee, which called for the new construction to be contained within a 40-story office tower. Our objective was to site the tower at the P & G complex establishing an appropriate rapport with their existing 11-story building. We worked along side the Rockefeller Center Development Corporation, who had been advising P & G for nearly a year, as did the other two architectural firms. We presented our proposal, and were then asked to travel to Cincinnati to meet with P & G Chairman, John Smale, and President, Brad Butler. At the meeting, Bill Pedersen and I elaborated on our firm's design philosophy and spoke about the needs of their employees, their work environment, the building's image in Cincinnati, and what opportunities P & G would have to give back to their city through the new construction. As we left the meeting, we really had no idea of where we stood. We were very confident with our presentation, and I was particularly impressed with P & G's "hands-on" approach—they were genuinely interested in our proposed process of designing and the more esoteric issues surrounding the project.

We were leaving the building for the airport when Brad Butler caught up to us in the lobby; he explained that he wanted us to have a good trip home, and then told us we had been selected as the architects for P & G's new corporate headquarters. I have since joked that Bill and I were so excited and relieved that we flew home to New York but without the plane. At that time, we were still a relatively young firm and, as a result, we saw this project as the commission of a lifetime.

We were intent on approaching the process with as much intensity and enthusiasm as expressed by our client. We presented several different alternatives to the tower scheme. John Smale did not respond well to our first six or seven schemes.

FIGURE 8-4
*Procter & Gamble
Consolidated World
Headquarters, Cincinnati,
OH. (Top) View from
public garden. (Bottom)
View from northeast
toward downtown
Cincinnati. Photos by J.
Pottle/Esto, courtesy of
Kohn Pedersen Fox
Associates.*

He was concerned that the designs did not provide a sense of unity between the old and new structures. He made it clear that the existing building would have to be totally integrated—he did not want it to appear, or its employees to feel, second-class. *His comments triggered Bill's final scheme,* which called for a large, public garden space to serve as the focal point to the entire complex. It gave equal footing to both the old and the new structures by unifying the newly created L-shaped complex and establishing a sense of place. The ceremonial entrance to the site was located at the base of twin 16-story towers that anchored the overall site and served as the eastern gateway to the city. The issue of domination by a single tower was resolved by the scale of the two smaller towers that worked much better with the existing P & G building and with the context of the city of Cincinnati.

In our experience with P & G, the overall success was due to their credit as much as our own. They were excellent clients because they demanded the best solution and took the needed time to work closely with us. We held bimonthly meetings with their project group, headed by Don Lowly, Senior Vice President, David Crafts, Vice President, and John Lehigh, Project Manager, where they tested and questioned everything we presented. We found their curiosity and commitment to thoughtful problem-solving inspiring. These characteristics were largely responsible for our intensive working meetings, where everybody, particularly John Smale, with their sleeves rolled-up, stayed late in the day in order to move the project forward. The comprehensive nature of this commission made it the kind that most firms could only dream about. We knew this was an extraordinary opportunity to work with an exceptional corporate client and I believe our accomplishments and the mutual high regard shared to this day demonstrate what can be accomplished with sensitivity, talent, dedication, and commitment.

Relationship with Client Also Means Relationship with a Community and Context

Our affiliation with the American Broadcasting Companies, Inc. has spanned 17 years and 16 commissions, including programming, master planning and feasibility studies, interior architecture, and nine building projects. ABC, like any other corporate entity, develops its facilities with success in mind; in most cases the priority concern is for financial success, but in the case of

ABC—New York, it has also been necessary to successfully compromise and integrate with the established neighborhood and community at large.

Their operation, occupying most of the block between 66th and 67th Streets and Central Park West and Columbus Avenue, is set in the midst of one of the city's more elegant residential areas. Its residents have consistently and properly fought to prevent the intervention of a major corporate presence in their once tranquil enclave. Our challenge with the ABC—New York projects has been to *respect the existing architectural context while establishing a strong visual corporate identity for ABC.*

At the same time, we have had to integrate complex programming requirements such as television studios, technical support, and office and production space, all the while working to win the approval of an influential community of upper-middle class professionals. All of the ABC building projects have been implemented *piece by piece,* where we have had to make use of a concept known as "checker board" expansion. It stresses *pre-planning,* where redevelopment is considered relative to the client's and the community's projected needs and business. Coordination of any needed demolition, construction, and move-in is arranged so that activities on and around the site are never interrupted. From what, on many occasions over the years seemed to be irreconcilable differences between the client and the community, we (ABC, the community, and KPF) were able to arrive at architectural solutions designed with the utmost of concern for the early twentieth-century architectural context of the neighborhood *and* the commercial needs of ABC.

The association of the commercial client and the architect is complex and nonexclusive; many other entities such as financial institutions, community boards, and planning and zoning commissions are involved with and effect the professional dealings. Often, the interests of the client do not coincide with those of all or even one of the other involved parties. In such cases, the architect must serve as "quarterback," with the challenge of trying to bring all the represented groups, with their wants and needs, into a realistic form of agreement without losing sight of the design issues at hand.

Building in our urban areas is particularly difficult. In general, people are resistant to change; negative responses are seemingly at every turn when attempting to add to the city, even if for the better. The need for more office space, though currently on hold

FIGURE 8-5
Various ABC–New York projects: Oblique view of ABC Phase II, Phase III (ABC/Capital Cities Headquarters), and Phase IV (ABC—Healy Building) from 66th Street looking west toward Columbus Avenue. Photo by J. Pottle/Esto, courtesy of Kohn Pedersen Fox Associates.

and probably remaining so well into the 1990s, will continue to cause new construction at some point in the future. Albeit subjective and difficult to quantify, good architecture has made a name for itself, and corporate executives and commercial developers know this. The benefits a well-designed building offers, such as addressing its surroundings, increasing employee productivity, enhancing the corporate image, and creating spaces and properties that will lease or sell at higher rates, are long-term.

When architects and commercial clients work together toward common goals and objectives, great things can happen in our cities, towns, and communities. 333 Wacker Drive illustrates how an intuitive developer, by taking a sizable speculative risk, added to, and in turn upgraded and enhanced a weak area of the core of Chicago. One Logan Square in Philadelphia, a group venture with profit-based building types as its focus, successfully integrated with the surrounding institutional setting to complete William Penn's classically inspired Logan Square. For the design of their new world headquarters in Cincinnati, the Procter & Gamble Company matched our every step in terms of commitment and intensity. Our long-term rapport with ABC demonstrates that designing specialized architecture for a corporate body in a densely urban residential environment, as improbable as that seems, can be accomplished to the benefit of all the parties involved.

Architecture is a multifaceted pursuit. It is not just external trimmings or a shell and a core. A building has to address numerous issues beyond its own enclosure. Most important, it needs to be responsive to the context in which it will stand. It must appeal to not only the needs of its users but to its streets, neighbors, history, and the community and city at large. Great commercial/corporate architecture is not always easy to come by. It is the result of the vision and willingness to risk of the developer and the talent, inspiration, enthusiasm, and execution of the architect, the client, and the community.

It's All in a Name

Thomas Bakalars' amusing tale about receiving a commission to convert an 1892 bank building into a headquarters for a prestigious, nonprofit organization is not only a model for adaptive reuse but an example of the impact of bureaucratic error on architect–client relations.

Mr. Bakalars is president and founder of Thomas Bakalars Architects, PC in Cambridge, MA. His work includes projects for some of the largest cinema corporations—Hoyts, Paramount, and General Cinema. The firm's residential and commercial work has been featured in Good Housekeeping, Variety, *and other professional and trade journals.*

It's 1985. I am a recent graduate of the Harvard Graduate School of Design called in by Henry Cobb [then Chairman of the Department of Architecture] to rewrite my review of a faculty member up for tenure (which is another story). As I dutifully recant, Mr. Cobb mentions that an organization called the Two/Ten Foundation is renovating a nineteenth-century bank building in Watertown, MA, and is looking for someone to do the design work. Would I be interested?

Fred Bloom is the one who actually hires me after an initial meeting. He is a professional fundraiser, still pushing his compact sixtyish body through endless rounds of lunches, dinners, and cocktail parties. He seems really happy, I mean *really* happy, to meet me. We talk for quite a while about modern art, which is an avocation of mine. Now, I didn't know this at the time, but Bloom is now convinced that I am some relation of David Bakalar, a significant patron of the arts in the Boston area.

The contract is a done deal before Bloom sits back and gives me a wink.

"So, how is your father?" he asks.

"My father?"

"Yes," he claps me on the back. "How is he?"

"Well, he's fine, thank you."

"And how is business?"

"Good. The market is looking up in Wisconsin." My father is a retired professor turned developer.

Bloom's face falls. "You're *not* related to David Bakalar?"

Well, what could I do?

The Two/Ten International Footwear Foundation, founded in 1939, is a privately funded nonprofit charity for the benefit of retailers, manufacturers, distributors, and importers of footwear. The Foundation's good works include social services, job placement assistance, and a popular scholarship program. Its original location was 210 Lincoln Street in Boston; hence the name.

The building they have acquired is very clean structurally, and very well maintained. The real issues are in space planning and furniture, finishes, and equipment. The 1892 bank building needs to be turned into offices; the existing furniture is a hodgepodge of ugly design spanning 20 or 30 years. Nothing matches and none of it presents the desired image. The budget I am originally presented with is modest, and I put in long hours working to squeeze the most out of every available dollar.

Meanwhile, Bloom and his band of fundraisers are making donation history. I eat out a lot during the schematic design phase, sitting at Bloom's side as he sweet-talks the wealthy mem-

FIGURE 8-6
The 4,400 square foot existing building for Two/Ten Charity Trust, Inc. is located in Watertown, MA. The design team's task involved an exterior restoration and interior rehabilitation of the entire structure. Drawing courtesy of Thomas Bakalars Architects PC.

bers. By the time he's through, the foundation has raised five times the budgeted amount for the project. Simple enough, the Board thinks—divert the excess into the scholarship fund or operating budget. Wrong, say the lawyers. The money has to be used on the building or it has to be returned.

Suddenly, this is a lavish project. Even after a generous building maintenance fund is established, I've got something like one million dollars to play with.

"Will you be able to spend the money?" the Board implores.

No problem.

"We don't want to appear ... ostentatious."

The renovation is all understated elegance. The exterior is restored to its original state (Figure 8-6); we replace the west bays and pediment that were removed in 1928. We resolve public sequencing and establish the cellular plan mandated by the Building Committee to facilitate donations (Figure 8-7). The remaining funds go to custom interior window and partition detailing, an elegant reception desk, display cases, recessed blinds,

Lower Level	1. Entry Hall
Main Level	2. Reception
Upper Level	3. Waiting Room
	4. Service Office
	5. Library
	6. Conference Room
	7. Executive Office
	8. Executive Conference
	9. Clerical
	10. Office Manager
	11. Staff Office
	12. Computer Room
	13. Employee Lunch Room
	14. Mechanical

FIGURE 8-7

The cellular nature of the plans was mandated by the Two/Ten Charity Trust Building Committee to facilitate donations for sponsorship of defined areas. Drawing courtesy of Thomas Bakalars Architects PC.

very durable fine furniture, etching on the mirror over the mantel, and on really nice plaques (slate with gold leaf, to be precise) identifying the major donors. Every room, every corridor, and every floor has a "Gift of" plaque. With furnishings, the cost per square foot comes in at 500 dollars.

The Open House when the project is completed is thrilling for me. This is my first built project. Kitty Dukakis is there, and I am appointed to give her a private tour. I discover that "private" is a relative term and that I can scarcely get a word in edgewise with the entourage tagging along with us. Finally, she turns to me and smiles, asking me to give her regards to Sandy.

Sandy?

Sandy Bakalar. You must be related? she asks.

Wouldn't you know Michael Dukakis dated Sandy Bakalar in high school? (She was Sandy Cohen back then.) Sandy set Michael and Kitty up on their first date! It's the mistaken identity thing all over again.

Later that night, a dinner for 400 is held in a hotel in downtown Boston. When Mel Sherman, the Chairman of the Board, introduces me, the audience gives me a standing ovation. Seeing all these heads of corporations and generally powerful people clapping for me, I am really looking forward to the rest of my career, let me tell you. I expected to sit back and let the skyscraper commissions roll in.

Well, nothing like that happened. As far as I can tell, I never got one lead out of that project. And that big budget, all that surplus funding? I renegotiated my fee as only a brand-new graduate could. I guess I earned about four dollars an hour.

CHAPTER 9

ALL PROJECTS GREAT AND SMALL

Just do it ... yourself. The phrase can evoke anything from the fitness of the long distance runner to five years of weekends fixing-up a back room. Much of this chapter examines the small scale project, and explores aspects of participation of both architects and clients in its design and construction. Apart from the vagaries of the spectrum of small projects, what links them all is an intensely personal, emotional, and idiosyncratic quality—one that must at least be recognized if not understood in order to achieve success.

Summer vacations (leaving client and builder *home alone—* without the architect), collecting fees, and personality-laden clients and character-rich spaces of independent bookstores round-out the material in this chapter.

Measure Twice, Cut Once
Architects and Aphorisms—
Therapy in the Spoken Word

*Architect Duo Dickinson's humor is clearly informed by many years
of experience working with clients and builders. In his wise and entertaining essay that follows, he captures the poetry and angst of the
day-to-day struggles of an architect.*

*Duo Dickinson, a Cornell University graduate, is principal of his
own five-person office in Madison, Connecticut. He has written four
books on architecture, the latest* Small Houses for the Next Cen-

tury, *was published by McGraw-Hill in 1994. Mr. Dickinson has taught at Yale College and Roger Williams University. His work has been featured in over 40 national and international magazines, including an* Architectural Record *House award for his own residence in 1985.*

"Measure twice, cut once."

If a television program can synopsize our willingness as a culture to substitute clichés for substance it is "This Old House." When architects watch this show (usually for vicarious thrills during a recession—at least we can *see* somebody building *something)*, they cringe at the lack of insight and innovation presented by all parties concerned—but especially by the architects as presented to the audience by the producers. At the appropriate moment their concerned faces spout sound-bites with just enough aphoristic clout to have the tiniest bit of resonance. The collective wit and wisdom of this program has been distilled to the "common sense" comment, "Measure twice, cut once." This quote has been emblazoned on millions of T-shirts and coffee mugs owned by Public Television elitists.

The real world of design and construction presents far more unpredictable, ambiguous, and just plain stupid vignettes. Televised craftsmanship is sterile when compared to the lack of pretense and self-imbued ego that are present when people of good will get together to build something. Witness the "anti-cliché" spouted to me by a carpenter with a vague smell of Miller on his breath on a hot summer job site at about 1:15 in the afternoon ...

"I've cut it three times and it's still too short."

Given the ups and downs and vagaries of the design/build process where the motivation to build things is seldom limited to the basic human need for shelter, and given the lack of a rule book to tell us exactly what to do at any given moment, there is a lot to be learned from the collected wisdoms of those who have distilled their humor and knowledge into *meaningful* sound-bites from which anyone can learn.

"I have a porch addition—and some smaller projects."

This quote has been ascribed to a young Michael Graves—an architect who presumably now looks upon porches as infinitesimal specks of graphite dust on gigantic plans for huge projects—elements that have now probably fallen from his consciousness.

But within this quote lies a subtle commentary about the latent outlook of most architects. We try to put our best foot forward and convince the world (and mostly ourselves) that there is actually a real, viable, professional future in designing things for people. "God is in the details" *especially* when *all* you have the opportunity to design is detail work.

It is this sort of gallows humor that provides architects and builders with some of their best lines. This attitude reminds me of a phrase from a 1974 *National Lampoon* magazine depicting a parody of a Pillsbury advertisement for its crescent rolls. In this case it was for "Nilsbury"—and showed the classic Dough Boy figure (but in this case with ribs showing) staring vacantly into an empty cardboard tube that once held crescent roll dough and supposedly murmuring the phrase ...

"Nothing says nothing like nothing from the oven."

As bleak as this is, it does allow us to laugh at a hopeless situation when there is very little in the real world that makes sense (darkly enough in this case the Biafran famine). So it can be with architecture. Phrases that are literally cynical become almost hopeful in their irony.

"Free advice and worth every penny."

So said a young architect/builder in giving a time-consumptive bid that I was extraordinarily grateful to receive. He put a spin on his services that allowed me to appreciate their *real* value despite all his hard work. In the construction industry, all professionals involved risk their time in trying to *get work* and clients are often all too willing to take advantage of this willingness to pick the brains of those who desperately want to execute their project. A valuable lesson to be learned from this young builder is that the budgeting and planning work that architects and builders do *before* things actually come out of the ground are inherently flawed and conceptual.

When I use this phrase to conclude my sales pitch to potential clients who are interviewing me, they often look blank and then giggle—realizing that I've acknowledged that any thoughts I give them with such limited data on a first blush basis are inherently incomplete and it would be silly of them to hold any view offered up in such a vacuum as anything other than a personal reaction. In this way, humor casts the bright light of truth on the presumptions of everyone concerned. It's humor born of experience that can guide architects and clients into understanding that the business of design has very little *tangible* value and a great deal of *perceived* value that is derived from experience, trust, and the indefinable belief that aesthetics have meaning.

"A good architect can turn a screw-up into a feature."

So spake architect David Sellers—someone who might describe himself as relatively "out there," beyond the world of architectural normalcy. His quote is the natural progression of the previous quote—merely that it is extraordinarily easy to offer up a design or an aesthetic construct based on imprecise data. Anything that exists on paper always *evolves* as it begins to become a physical reality. There are often extraordinarily lyric and poignant architectural elements that evidence the greatest level of skill because they *compensate* for something that was completely unanticipated.

A flowing stair that I executed in a project in New York could be said to be curvilinear counterpoint to an angular context—inserting lush ash and walnut steps into a preexisting world of unfinished redwood—but in truth we saved 20,000 dollars by *not moving* a 400-amp electrical power box (discovered once we removed part of the house that surrounded it). Should we have known that power box was there before demolition? In the best of all possible worlds, yes. Does the final product look like we did not anticipate that potentially costly feature? Hopefully not.

"Good, fast, and cheap—you can only have two—the third is always excluded."

Think about it—if a project is "good" (high quality, lustrous materials) and "fast" (executed quickly) it involves the highest level of skill and resources, and is always relatively costly—it *won't* be "cheap."

If a project is "fast" and "cheap," odds are it *won't* be "good."

If a project is "good" and "cheap" it almost always takes a *long* time to execute—skill levels are low, or there is little or no "organization" behind the construction—hence it *won't* be "fast."

Since a builder revealed this construct to me, it has been claimed by clients of mine who are in advertising and other industries involving money and schedules.

More money can save time and facilitate quality. *More* time can compensate for less money. These are simple truths that provide perspective beyond the 1980s cliché, "You can't have it all."

"It'll get done before it's too late."

So said a hardwood sawmill owner to stairmaker Richard Walston. He'd asked for a *date* when he could pick up his material—having waited months when weeks were quoted. When asked how *long* he'd have to wait "before it's too late," Walston was asked:

"How long is a piece of string?"

Building anything that has *not* been built before makes timing and costs virtually incalculable in any finite terms. Rather than let the angst get you down, these vagaries are used to spawn humor that is both cautionary and therapeutic.

Words and architecture don't mix very well. Architects are infamous for obfuscatory polysyllabic nomenclature (and I just proved it!). So it's often left to these seemingly jaded phrasings to capture the true essence of what makes architecture so tough to describe—both as art and as a profession.

"There are three rules of architecture: (1) get the job, (2) get the job, and (3) get the job."

This has been ascribed to architect Vincent Kling of Philadelphia, but it conveys (not unlike the three rules of real estate, "location, location, and location") a universal truth. In this case the point is if you design without clients and are without work to *build* you are a dilettante. An architect *builds* by "getting the job;" a dilettante makes excuses, feels bitter, and does not practice architecture so much as conceptual art. Without "jobs" to execute, there is no *architecture*—only aesthetic ideas that may (or may not) apply to building something.

Architectural theory constantly flails about, trying to locate its hard edge (or edges). Definition of aesthetic theory is akin to catching spring water in your cupped hands—you get only a little of it and it's never easy to hold on to. Aphorisms invalidate the pretensions of the theoretical by casting the bright light of a reality on fuzzy concepts often based on nonarchitectural values set amid personal jealousies. The more we expose pretense the thinner the emperor's garments become.

AS DRAWN

1. INCREASE ROOF PITCH TO 8 IN 12

2. HAVE FUN WITH EAVE TRIM

3. ACCENTUATE THE DOOR/ADD WINDOW

4. ADD A "LEGIT" STOOP

5. ADD LIGHTING

6. MAKE THE BOTTOM EDGE "SPECIAL"

7. REALITY CHECK

8. FINAL DESIGN

FIGURE 9-1
Images showing the progression between a builder's sketch and the final design for an outbuilding in New Canaan, CT. In some respects these sketches present an answer to the cliché query, "Why the hell hire an architect, anyway?" That's the way I used them when the client came to me and asked, "Does it make sense to hire you?" I responded, "No job too small, no fee too high," and proceeded to transform the builder's rude image into a semiexpressive little box.

Less May Actually Be More: The Politics of the Small Project

Architect Joe Harris has said, "What sets successful architects apart is producing a good concept within the confines of the opportunity an owner has given them." This is a profound statement in view of the following four projects, all tiny *in scale and low-cost, and each for a very distinctive client.*

The opportunities presented by the clients in these stories, were, in fact, huge. Each client was eager to empower the architect with creative control at the outset, along with a set of needs and preferences. Once the program was set, including functional requirements and general intent, the architect was free to design, unencumbered by changes or questions along the way.

In most cases an ongoing dialogue between architect and client is not only politically or diplomatically desirable but crucial to the creativity in developing the most responsive schemes for tough challenges. (This is perhaps why design competitions, in general, are severely flawed—no communication and no give-and-take between designer and client are allowed during the design process.) When considering architecture applied to residential work at the scale of a room, a playhouse, a kitchen, or an entry, all within a modest budget, the design process must be further adjusted. An architectural consultation, to develop concepts and to suggest the general means of implementation is probably the best (and the only practical) utilization of both the professional's time and the client's dollar. In other words, consultation as opposed to comprehensive services is the most efficient, effective, and politically manageable approach in the small project realm. Michael Crosbie, a leading architectural journalist, affirms this sentiment by stating that it's time architects surrendered their all-or-nothing design ethic (epitomized by Howard Roark in The Fountainhead). *Crosbie believes, "The trouble is, we're trained to get a death grip on a project and wrestle it away from the client ... architects should be more helpful."*

There is a surprising level of design and meaning in the architecture to be created from small projects. With great ease and passion, we all throw ourselves into the big, high-profile jobs; it's surely axiomatic that we also tend to disdain the ordinary and relatively small endeavor. Mundane little projects, however, may loom very large for those of us who will live with them. *The following case illustrations demonstrate some of the typical feelings of, and interactions among client and architect both struggling toward their common good.*

(I) Making an Entrance

*"All the world's a stage,
And all the men and women merely players:
They have their exits and their entrances..."*

—William Shakespeare

It was bad enough working late and having to negotiate a particularly intense Beltway that night. Then, to find herself unable to recognize the place she had lived for this past year was something else again. With a thin cover of snow and minimal street lighting, every house in the new suburban subdivision seemed identical. The row of standardized façades by day blurred into a block-long monolith by night.

More from habit than visual cue, home was identified. Fumbling with her keys and the alarm system in the ever darkening evening, our heroine took a step up as she pushed open the front door. At the same time, she slipped on the frozen slush, and briefcase and purse went flying into the Maryland night.

So went the story of Matilda Wu, a young lawyer whose campaign preparations for State Representative had been somewhat thwarted by a small assortment of fractured limbs and ribs.

Matilda sat at my conference table, crutches to her left, leather trimmed backpack on the floor to her right. With a very serious expression, she summarized: "I want to be able to find my house in the middle of the night when I'm very tired and preoccupied, and in bad weather I want my front steps protected, and whatever you do, it *can't* be distinctive: I want to preserve my anonymity; I certainly don't want the house to stick out like a sore thumb."

I commented, "Mmm—bold yet demure, tall yet short, omnipresent yet somehow absent." Fortunately, Matilda cracked a smile and replied, "Yea, that sounds about right." (Humor is sometimes *the* most valuable political device.)

I reassured Matilda that I could offer a happy ending for her all too common story. With its potentials for both functionally and aesthetically transforming a façade, the modestly scaled entry is, ironically, perhaps the single most powerful residential addition that can be undertaken.

Matilda continued to detail her goals for the project: "I do want more than a cute little nose job on the face of the house, and I do want something more than an unobtrusive bit of shelter with storage for a snow shovel. I want a real place of transition— from which I gear up for 'big entrances' into the political arena on the way to work, and then collapse back into when I'm ready to return home. Just walking up Independence Avenue, you know, with the Capitol on the left and the House office buildings on the right, and all the young-ambitious, and the old-powerful striding and strolling—it's exhilarating and scary at the same time, and I'll tell you, it requires some kind of performance to navigate the day. Before I moved here from San Francisco, I visited the District a lot, and my firm would always get me a room at the Mayflower or the Willard. When you walk out of those lobbies, well, you're somehow prepared, energized, walking The Walk, you know what I mean?"

I said, "Of course. You want your entry to give you a cue, to signal the change of ambiance, to help you take a deep breath and let it out slowly, to turn on the right mental tapes, all as you leave to face the day and make the move on stage." (A good politician not only understands the constituency, but also helps the constituency to *feel* understood.)

"That's it," Matilda said. "That's exactly it, and I appreciate your application of the stage metaphor. Then after I've survived the matinee and perhaps an evening show as well, I want to be able to come home and reverse the process."

I tried to clarify further, "You mean, get the cue for warming-down and becoming yourself again."

"Yes, something like that, like a lobby that now says, 'time for a change of pace:' You can cease being brilliant and glamorous, and put on sweats, and go get a bowl of Haagen-Dazs."

I now had to comment about harsh reality: "Obviously, you can't have the lobby of an elegant hotel—the scale, the opulent finishes, the feelings of calm and power. I can certainly avoid designing an addition that looks like a restaurant kitchen exhaust vent, and I may be able to realize some of the very genuine potentials for a residential entry—it will undoubtedly be a place of transition—we're good at integrating sculptural form, storage areas, materials, even plants. But, it's too easy to get carried away."

In a role reversal that was a first for me, Matilda insisted that her project *"was not to be trivialized,"* and might in fact hold even more promise than I could ever imagine. She said, "You've got me intrigued and ready to spend some money—don't destroy my dreams!"

I replied, "I merely want to suggest that expectations remain in the realm of practical possibilities. I certainly reach for the theoretical ideal, but," I searched for the right words, "In politics, you wouldn't want to make a speech in which you identify all kinds of idealistic goals and imply a promise that you'll deliver. You promise you'll do your best to *try* to deliver on those

FIGURE 9-2

(Left) "Before"—A rather dull, flat façade with a front door fully exposed to the elements. (Right) "After"—As a natural extension of the original house, the entry adds a third dimension that strengthens the natural focus on the front door, and provides protection from wind, rain, and snow. A transition between inside and outside, the new entry was conceived as an outdoor foyer with concealed glare-free lighting, room for plants, and a built-in mailbox. Side walls can be oversized to incorporate storage cabinets, planters, and benches. An added trellis offset from the wall can blend the boundary between the landscape and the house. Design and Drawings by Andy Pressman.

goals, right? I think that architecture is probably similar to politics in this regard. I've been upset too many times because it's so easy to pledge everything and sometimes even deliver—and then the client fires you because in his or her mind, even the goals and promises suddenly appear alien. So, please don't get me wrong; all I ask is that we all agree on some rather simple, concrete goals, and if we exceed our hopes, then we've all collaborated to produce a little magic—that is, architecture."

The final design for the entry turned out to be modest, buildable, and pleasing to the client. Several years and elections later, Congresswoman Wu remains happy with her entry. I suppose we actually did produce a little magic after all, and in no small way because of an enlightened and energetic political transaction.

(II) Do-It-Yourself

Friends of friends referred a nice couple in their early forties to me. Harvey and Patrice were established as physical therapists with their own practice. They had three boys who ranged from four to eight years of age. The two family cars never saw the garage, which was filled with bicycles, toys, pet paraphernalia, and residuals of skiing and barbecuing.

With the children's arrival at the school and wild growth and development phases, Harvey and Pat realized that they needed more space. The couple came to me with this problem, and another: "We have no money right now." Unlike some who say the words and then spend tens of thousands of dollars on renovation or addition, Harvey and Pat actually had little more than 1500 dollars "to play with."

Our mutual friends had talked about me as being creative and able to stretch a budget, and Harvey was more than half-serious about devising some kind of storage tent in the back yard. In her resulting panic, Pat insisted that they at least present their problem to me and see what I might propose.

Pat would turn out to be the key to the success of this project in more ways than just seeing to it that an architect was involved. She immediately volunteered herself as general contractor, saying, with a little tongue-in-cheek, "I do everything else around here, why not carpentry too?"

I was certainly interested, and Harvey seemed somewhat relieved. He related a comical but nightmarish dream in which he was totally alone in a do-it-yourself theme park. Unfinished and obviously botched home handyman projects surrounded him. The devil, looking like Bob Vila, appeared and commanded Harvey to complete the entire array of projects, otherwise he would remain in the park for eternity. Harvey felt he had already developed a classic case of "construction performance anxiety."

Pat went on to speculate that the possibility for involving the children in the construction seemed attractive from a number of standpoints: It would help keep them busy, maybe they would learn a bit about teamwork, acquire a few skills, and derive satisfaction from seeing the results of their work. Moreover, their involvement in the early stages of any project might ensure that they would take better care of the final product.

The concept for the project emerged as a playhouse for the kids that could do double-duty as storage space for yard tools, outdoor furniture, and so on. The element we strived to develop was the fantasy clubhouse feeling that seems to drive the best imaginative play. I recalled my childhood wanderings among the fabulous playhouses on display at F.A.O. Schwarz in New York City. After some happy reminiscing, we conceived a plywood castle with balcony, parapet, ladder, gates, arches, grand hall, window, and sand parlor. It was to rest on concrete pier blocks, and sit up against a rear wall of Harvey and Pat's house, looking out at the full expanse of back yard.

FIGURE 9-3
Sketches of the fantasy playhouse: A multilevel plywood castle that doubles as storage for yard equipment. It is intended to elicit imaginative play, and provide a visual lesson in geometry, space, and scale. Design and drawings by Andy Pressman.

FIGURE 9-4
The built work has a central interior space (a simple shed), and is flanked by a sandbox and a tower with balcony accessible by ladder. Big arches and squares are easy to cut out of 5/8-inch plywood panels that wrap the shed. Masonry block is used as an apron in front of the shed doors to extend the play area into the yard when doors are open. Design by Andy Pressman. Photo © Chris Eden/Eden Arts.

A WORD ON THE PITFALL OF "PC"

As excited as I was about this little exercise (and the associated local publicity), there was something else gnawing at me. It was not so much about this particular project, but about what it came to represent or misrepresent. I felt that the entire do-it-yourself movement was great except when it becomes so "politically correct" that there is a blindspot for *craftsmanship and craftspeople.* Simply and resolutely deciding to wallpaper your kitchen or install a tile floor is a far cry from accomplishing those tasks with a special competence and flair that may actually "touch the soul," as Charles Moore has said. Much of the enthusiasm for do-it-yourself home improvement is undoubtedly influenced by the economy, and we all must do what is necessary to get by—but it is presumptuous to foster the belief that the handiwork we young urban professionals may do is anywhere near the quality of that which professional craftspeople are capable. Talent, training, apprenticeship, and experience are special commodities and we should respect the results.

(III) Good Guest Rooms Make Good Guests

George was pleased with himself. He had completed the mission: He had met the challenge of scooping-up his mother-in-law from the North Terminal. As he accelerated into the south-bound traffic, his passenger turned and smiled. Things were going well this time—then, without warning, the spell was broken: "George, will I be staying in the sunroom again? You know, that cot you have does give me such a backache. And the kids' toys, do you know how many times I've tripped and nearly fallen over that stuff? And I feel so self-conscious trooping upstairs to use your bathroom. I don't mean to be difficult, George, but you really should do something—especially now that I'm a *Frequent Flyer*."

The crowd roared as George sprinted the last 100 meters of the race. He would be the oldest Olympic gold medalist in history. Suddenly, he was pushed hard from his left. Opening his eyes, George saw his wife's face and heard her say, "Wake-up, you're kicking me!"

"Oh, sorry, I'm sorry," he responded, breathless. George's wife had collapsed back to sleep and George, try as he might, could not follow suit. So, he decided to do what any typical American male would, he started toward the kitchen. Through the bedroom door and one stride into the living room, he remembered the cousins. Too late. Catching his right foot on a corner of the futon that was unfolded on the floor, George went sprawling, bouncing first off one sleeping cousin, then the other. Barney, the Sheepdog, began barking maniacally and rushed headlong toward what he thought was the clear path to safety under George's bed.

George reflected on how much he loved Sunday mornings— *The New York Times,* fresh bagels, and above all, peace—delicious, calm, quiet, leisurely. The harsh buzz of the doorbell violently intruded on George's reverie. He stood and reluctantly made his way to the front door.

"George! How the hell are ya? Well, c'mon, ask us in— where's the Gatorade?"

George stared for a second in silence at the sight before him: Two of his closest and most dreaded old college buddies— perched on bright red mountain bikes with full packs on their backs.

"Listen, babe, let us bunk here, just for the night and we'll cook you a dinner just like at Kappa Sig, whad'ya say, huh?"

George called me on a Monday morning with a plea to help preserve his sanity, his marriage, and his family. He wanted to convert an underused sunroom into a guest room with bath. George felt as though he *always* had guests, but was aware that most of the time, his children used the sunroom as an all-purpose area. The question was whether or not the old space could be transformed into a guest suite. At the same time, it would still need to be able to function as the multipurpose play room for the kids (aged three to seventeen) when there were no house guests. I assured George that these were indeed achievable goals, and that both his family and sanity were likely to remain intact.

FIGURE 9-5

(Left) Sketch illustrating platforms of varying heights and a soffit with new recessed lighting. A twin-size mattress above storage drawers doubles as a couch and bed for the occasional overnight guest. Perimeter illumination comes from incandescent fixtures tucked behind the fascia board that ties into the soffit. Design and drawing by Andy Pressman. (Right) Storage is everywhere: In this view into the bathroom, access doors under the towel rack capture space underneath a platform. Photo by Greg Sharko, © Times Mirror Magazines, Inc.

(IV) Cooking with Design

The little Southwest Airlines 737 skidded and bumped its way through 20,000 feet. As we descended—rather quickly, I might add—the Sandia Mountains loomed large through the windows on the right side of the airplane. My usual flying headache escalated with the rate of descent, and any awareness I might have had of the approach into Albuquerque was quite muted.

When the old Boeing finally came to a stop, I pushed toward the front door as fast as etiquette permitted. I needed air ASAP. The crispness of the fresh air and the vividness of the colors actually began to relieve the pain in my head. I shouldered my carry-on bag, marched down the exit stairs, and made my way through the airport. National Guard F-4 Phantoms streaked across the desert as I picked up my Hertz Escort and pointed the hood toward Santa Fe.

As I drove North on I-25, I reviewed what I knew about the client. Billie Campbell, an artist and Navajo activist, was referred to me by one of my contacts at the Department of the Interior. She was described as "bright, gifted, and perhaps too passionate to be very effective as a politician." Flying-in to design her kitchen seemed comically trivial as well as inefficient, but my friend at the Department of the Interior insisted that he would "owe me big." Anyway, I was ready for a change, and this opportunity seemed like a good way to begin a brief vacation.

Everything in Santa Fe, from fastfood places to the exquisite historic buildings, emulated the Spanish-Pueblo style of adobe and wood construction. In contrast to the warmth and apparent age of the city were the cold purple hues of the jagged peaks of the Sangre de Cristo Mountains. I found my hotel, checked-in, and began to anticipate the next morning's meeting with Ms. Campbell.

"Located amid the greatest repository of human memory in North America, the Program for Indian Arts would invite close, successful contact between students and visiting artists and mainstream society in a rich and truly Indian framework. We can utilize our culture as a medium for outreach—as a means of channeling and educating the energies of youth on the reservations. We need your help now. Give generously. Thank you."

I clapped vigorously in concert with the rest of the crowd assembled in the small exhibit space of the Institute of American Indian Arts. Billie Campbell was indeed a passionate individual, and, from my glances about the gallery, a compelling painter. Here I stood, a struggling architect, about to design a *damn kitchen*. Suddenly, this vacation was not helping my carefully justified and tenuous professional self-image.

Without figuring out how to reconcile the kitchen with my own need to do something socially meaningful, I introduced myself to Ms. Campbell. She greeted me politely and with appropriate enthusiasm, and suggested we talk over coffee in her home on Canyon Road. The house was a 10 minute drive from the Institute. We parked in an elongated oval space dusted with bleached gravel and sand. A six-foot high garden wall marked the beginning of Campbell's property and created a private courtyard, beyond which sat a modestly scaled but beautifully proportioned home.

Inside, it was instantly apparent that Billie Campbell had not only already selected manufactured kitchen cabinets, but had them delivered as well. Boxes were stacked in the living room and kitchen, and a few seemed to tumble into the adjoining studio. The kitchen itself was a mess, and underneath various appliances, it seemed rather unfinished.

When a client has already made irrevocable decisions, then the architectural task is rather haphazardly narrowed. There is a loss of control over the big picture, and it is more difficult to explore and demonstrate what may be possible. Looking on the positive side, the more difficult the constraints, the greater the need for creative thinking, and the greater the satisfaction if the project turns out at all well.

"You know," Billie said, casually waving at the piles of boxes, "I saw these same cabinets at my boyfriend's shop, and figured I would get a head start."

"Mm hmm," I replied.

Billie came back with what seemed slightly sarcastic, "So, Ray (our mutual acquaintance) tells me you're the rescuer of all good kitchens gone bad?"

"When you put it that way," I answered, "it sounds as if I belong in a gothic romance novel. But yes, I have recently attacked kitchens, family rooms, and back porches with some success."

Billie Campbell then all but leapt upon my loose comment: "Am I to take it that you're less than thrilled to be here? You know there are a dozen local people, including three Indian architects I could have approached."

I collected myself and said, "Look, Ms. Campbell, I didn't mean it that way. Like you, however, I see myself as trying to be an activist wherever possible, and your talk back at the Institute had an impact. I will admit to feeling a bit guilty about engaging work that someone once described as 'more socialite than socialist.' And, I'll bet you'd want your architect to think just that."

Billie Campbell shook her head, silently clapping her hands in mock applause. We were back in business.

After I'd completed taking measurements of the space and compiling an inventory of what Billie purchased, the two of us finally sat down for the promised cup of coffee. Apart from design, this was the aspect of being an architect I consistently found most interesting: Sitting with a client and promoting a little self-revelation in order to gain a feeling for what he or she really wants. Once in a great while, this task is startlingly easy. Such was the case with Billie Campbell. A more psychologically minded individual was rare, and her multimedia capacity for self-expression made her all too transparent.

Only several sips into her coffee, and seconds into the answer to my initial probe about the timing of her kitchen project, Billie opened her soul: "You know, it's funny. I tend to work in the kitchen."

I smiled.

"No, really. Not just my writing, but I paint here. For now, I moved all my things into the studio, but the bulk of my work that's not actually done in the desert is created right here. I love this space."

"So, all your good works are completed in the kitchen?"

"Exactly. That's it—*completed.* And the one thing I can't get off the ground, much less complete, is my most important work."

"The Program for Indian Arts," I interjected.

Billie went on, "It's been three years since I began the crusade. It just seems stuck. Everyone cheers and is excited and then the Board of Trustees can't agree to approve the funds—money that is already sitting in the Reservation treasury—that's the tragedy. So, I'm now in the position of a fund-raiser and my audience is white."

"I don't understand," I said. "There's no ambiguity that your Program is likely to be of great benefit to your people."

Billie smiled sardonically and said, "Of course not, but that's not the issue. Half the board is composed of very angry young men who will do anything to avoid facilitating intercultural dialogue; their purpose is to preserve and even energize barriers between our societies—they believe that is the only way to achieve a healthy Indian self-esteem."

Before I had a chance to really temper my words, I blurted out, "So, if you're stalled with the Program, at least you can complete your kitchen!"

To my amazement, Billie did not register disgust. Instead, she seemed to soften. Looking right at me, she said, "Thanks for understanding."

FIGURE 9-6

The built project. New beams reinforce a path through the kitchen to the back door. This path became the major organizing element for the entire space: There is a U-shaped work area on one side, and an alcove for appliances, countertop, and pantry on the other side. The beams add warmth and texture to the raw space, suggesting the intimacy of a lowered ceiling while maintaining a feeling of openness. Design by Andy Pressman. Photo © Steinkamp/Ballogg.

FIGURE 9-7
A more costly alternative: Demolition of a wall would have allowed additional space to be captured for a work area within the kitchen. The soffits, cabinets, and counter all work together to "step" in three dimensions, defining the proposed new focus for the space. Napkin skecth by Andy Pressman.

With her usual composure again, but without the edge, Billie spoke: "Dumb as it may sound, completing this little personal project is something I need to do, something I *can* control. And it's a distraction too—a way I can escape and renew a bit. So you see, Mr. Architect, you are not only designing me a respectable kitchen, but you are saving me from spending a lot of money on therapy!"

When Clients Think They're Architects and Other Tales of Woe

Roger K. Lewis, FAIA, concludes his contribution to The Fountainheadache *with a series of brief tales and accompanying "morals" that can be appreciated by architect and client alike. (The biography for Roger Lewis appears in "The Hospitable Tunisians" in Chapter 4.)*

When Clients Think They're Architects

It's among an architect's worst nightmares.

The large house was being framed and sheathed when I left for my summer vacation far up the Maine coast. A few days after my departure, the client, a couple with whom I had worked for over a year designing the house, called and informed me that they and the construction contractor had decided to make a small modification, one that they were certain was of no consequence and that I could readily accept. It concerned the fenestration.

To save money, both in material and labor costs, they had agreed in my absence to substitute a pair of windows at each of several locations on the façades where I had shown an ensemble of four windows. Who would notice the difference? The two windows would contain about the same amount of glass and occupy about the same overall area, they reasoned, as the quartet of windows called for in my meticulously studied elevation compositions. It seemed to them to be such a subtle distinction.

And by the way, my client said, the contractor already had done the work—framed the openings and bought and installed the windows. They just thought I should know about it before I returned from Maine. I gagged, expressed my concern, and then resigned myself to another aesthetic compromise. After all those months developing and refining the design, those countless hours spent explaining concepts and compositional details, my clients still didn't get it. And, practical souls that they are, they probably never will. It didn't completely spoil my vacation.

MORAL
Architects should carefully time their vacations so that clients and contractors are not left alone together.

Promises

Another client had paid us for the first couple of months, but now he owed us $17,000 for the most recent month when the bulk of the work, a master planning study, had been done. From that point on, I was told every story in the book. The check is in the mail. The money will be in the bank next week. New financing is about to be consummated. New partners are about to sign on. Any day now. Papers await execution. Wait just a few more days.

I waited for months. He was always amiable and apologetic and, incredibly, always sounded sincere and convincing. Finally, after repeated demands, he sent a check, a partial payment, but said not to cash it until he called. He never called. More time passed. The check was worthless. Finally, he agreed to give me a confessed judgment note, still imploring me not to worry and assuring me that payment in full was imminent. When the note came due, he defaulted. I hired an attorney who obtained the judgment and recorded a lien against the property. Nevertheless, all I had was a piece of paper.

After another year or two, I wrote off the $17,000 judgment as uncollectible and soon forgot about it. Therefore, it was nothing less than astounding when, over 10 years later, I received a call from the collection attorney—I had even forgotten his name—informing me that I soon would receive full payment on the note and judgment. The land had just been sold and, to clear title, my lien had to be satisfied. I would receive the entire principal amount, $17,000, plus years of accrued interest, less legal fees. The check arrived. And it didn't bounce.

MORAL
Sometimes it pays to wait, but, even better, it helps to have a lien against the client's property.

Vapor Lock

The circulating hot water heating system in our new, low-income housing project never worked properly. Several apartments just didn't get enough heat and sometimes got none. For nearly two years, no one could ascertain the cause with certainty—not us, the architects, not the contractor and subcontractor, not one of several independent mechanical engineering consultants called in to evaluate the problem. The mechanical engineer who had designed the system thought it was the pump installation and blamed the subcontractor and operators. The subcontractor insisted that he had constructed the system as designed. And the owner, a municipality, just wanted someone, whoever it might be, to take responsibility for finding and implementing a permanent remedy. The town's position was quite reasonable.

The flaw was finally discovered. There were no relief valves installed at high points in the circulating water line to release entrapped air. Intermittent vapor lock was blocking the flow of hot water. And sure enough, no such air bleeding valves were called for in the drawings and specifications. It was a design omission by our mechanical engineer. In the meantime, he had moved to another region of the country, was uninsured, and refused to take any financial responsibility for the error. As the architect, I alone was left holding the proverbial bag. The municipal officials knew that I was not personally at fault, but they also knew that I was insured.

The town demanded arbitration under the AIA Owner-Architect contract, and, pursuant to the usual negotiations, my insurance company settled and paid for the repairs. To collect anything from my engineering consultant would have required my filing a separate lawsuit, which was not worth the trouble. In the end, it personally cost me my deductible—5000 dollars—and a lot of time and aggravation. But the town got its system repaired.

MORAL
Don't assume that mechanical engineers know what they're doing.

Room without a View

According to Commercial Renovation *magazine, over 100,000 retail outlets are projected for renovation in 1993–1994, at a cost of 13 billion dollars to upgrade and "modernize" their existing properties. There will likely be significant impacts upon the construction industry and upon consumer behavior in the improved retail settings.*

A subset of store owners undertaking major changes in physical appearance for their very survival are the independent booksellers. These owners are a fascinating group: They are entertaining the public with a bottom-line purpose, and they seem uniquely committed to making their stores reflect the cultural and intellectual nature of their product. The designs they commission are intended to be fashionable, yet often express something very personal and unique, and therefore attract more customers. Sheila Wilensky-Lanford, owner of Oz Books in Southwest Harbor Maine, exemplifies the mind set: "I love the books, order the books, read the books, and touch the books. I love to connect the books with the people I know."

Competition from chain- and super-stores has forced bookstore owners to become partners with their architects, to work together against the common enemy. It is this kind of political context that translates to predisposition toward successful collaboration between architect and client.

The following three stories exemplify the clients' potential for identifying and communicating their own niche and strengths. Armed with this information, the challenge for the architect then becomes translating the goals to dramatic physical designs without spending a lot of money on what are usually leased spaces.

Southwest Harbor, Maine

I decided to take a friend on the scenic drive along coastal US Route 1 from Portland to my new client—Oz Books—located in one of the prettiest rural vacation resort towns in the state of Maine. To break-up the three-hour drive, I couldn't resist pulling into the parking lot of the Miss Stroudwater Truck Stop, near Brunswick.

"This is where you're taking me for brunch?" The hint of horror in Sue's tone might have been for real as she was no doubt expecting one of the more mainstream bed and breakfasts. But the scene was so great, so much like I remembered from childhood vacations, I parked.

We entered the diner to an overture of tractor-trailer diesels resonating at idle, amid splotches of neon signage. It was almost Norman Rockwell: The old sagging plank floor on its eighth or ninth coat of brown paint, the booths, and the stools at the counter were classic. I guided Sue, who appeared as if she was trying hard not to breathe, to a booth at the end, away from the crowd. Immediately, freckled, white fat hands delivered mugs of coffee, setting them on the faded-blue Formica counter.

This stop at a local hang-out was more than just nostalgic. The owner of Oz Books had insisted I get a sense of "the low-keyed small community feeling." She wanted me to design an expansion to her childrens' bookstore that was "magical, warm, exciting, and friendly," but more important, *"wasn't too fancy."* And I should be able to do this "for someone like me who thinks 100 dollars is a lot of money."

Getting something for nothing is usually part of the design challenge in most of my projects; but to pull it off in a case such as this, the client must have complete faith and trust in the abilities of the architect. Small construction budgets usually mean small design fees, so my cost-effective consultation typi-

FIGURE 9-8
View upon entering the childrens' bookstore. The arched reading alcove at the rear, scaled for kids, is an immediate magnet. Design by Andy Pressman. Photo © Robert Darby.

FIGURE 9-9
The centralized pavilion provides a new focus for the expanded store. Soffits with integral indirect lighting are supported by columns of book shelves. Design by Andy Pressman. Photo © Robert Darby.

cally involves a set of "implementation documents" sufficient to build the project. They usually do not include a three-dimensional representation, and even though relatively simple and straightforward, many clients have difficulty reading and understanding two-dimensional drawings. This is where faith and effective communication must predominate.

How things get done in the town was another more political issue: Who builds what, who coordinates the work, and who makes decisions during construction when the out-of-town architect can't come up for a field visit. The client was instrumental in identifying the various talented resource people. It was my job to orchestrate their involvement—who would be appropriate to contribute in terms of the special design features of this project. For example, all new book display fixtures would be fabricated by a good-quality manufacturer in another state. The pavilion in the center of the store, above the sales desk and main circulation aisle, would be built by a local carpenter. The new flooring, though not in accordance with the original design (I specified a wide strip of wood along the main entry axis, terminating in an arched reading nook), was all carpet, selected and purchased by the owner from a local distributor.

Working in a small town, with a very limited budget, and with the mandate for a bold design were all interesting constraints. And, to my surprise, working within and around these constraints proved feasible and more gratifying than I could ever imagine. A connection with the community, the region, and with the industry that the client represented, together was more satisfying than the completed project itself. My feeling was that derived from providing a "service" in contrast to an isolated product.

Valparaiso, Indiana
This bookstore, in the Hoosier State, also involved a renovation and expansion into an adjacent space. The client was distinctive in her sensitivity and political responsiveness to staff needs. She solicited their opinions from the outset, continued to ask for feedback, and made sure I heard what they had to say.

Driving from Chicago on Interstate 90 east during a lake-effect winter snow squall required my full attention to avoid becoming one with the blur of rubber and steel of the trucks that, in concert, appeared to be the size of nearby Gary, IN. Daydreaming about design possibilities was out of the question in this circumstance. So for better or worse, I arrived at the store for my first meeting without any preconceptions.

I was greeted by the owner, Susan Schenone, and her husband. They explained how they were able to interest a local business college to conduct surveys of customer attitudes—another unusual and clever strategy to fine-tune their proposed new design—this time from the customers' point of view. Schenone reiterated her comments that first appeared in a recent *Publishers Weekly* article: "The study said that it was awfully tight in here, and that one woman wouldn't even come in if she saw more than a couple of lingering customers." She continued, "We have to return to our original mission—to make the store a comfortable place to browse for books."

Achieving a balance between packing in as many books as possible and allowing pockets of space for leisurely browsing is critically important, fairly obvious, and often overlooked—particularly when there is rapid or on-going growth. An uninspired layout of display fixtures, gradually added to over the years, may present a maximum number of books but may not generate maximum sales. The point is that the character and quality of the space are just as important as efficiency; these are not mutually exclusive goals.

A concept for The Book Bag was to design a cost-effective intervention—one that was targeted to a particular area within the store to yield the biggest impact. This translated to an indoor pergola, a modest structure extending from the entry to the sales desk. While modulating the overwhelming proportions of the high ceiling and creating a more human scale, it would serve as an entry gallery for displays. Thoughts of Peter Eisenman's spectacular axis of white scaffolding for the Wexner Center at Ohio State jumped in my mind as a precedent, even though the scale nor the mission quite matched.

Annual sales for both The Book Bag and Oz Books have increased by 30 percent. The bottom line? Good design, active client participation, rapport with all involved parties, and a little luck make for satisfying architectural service.

Champaign, Illinois

The big, black rubbery nose of the Old English Sheepdog was mounted on a smiling, fuzzy snout, which in turn was attached to a great fluffy head. This was connected to a body—a shaggy, tail-less mass of good-natured dumbness, an endearing quality that is typical of the breed.

"Isaac! Come here boy!" Steve, my client, raised his voice, commanding the animal.

Isaac loped over probably thinking how graceful and petite he was. Miscalculating, he put brakes on a bit too late, and crashed into my legs, his rear-half still wagging in the excitement of greeting a stranger. A massive paw plopped on my knee, asking to be shook. A hand-to-paw exchange with this noble creature was perhaps worth my entire fee for the bookstore project that I was about to undertake: What a showcase of textures, forms, and sweetness.

Sweetness, however, is not how I would describe my relationships with the principal parties involved in developing one of the larger bookstores in the state. The major problem was that my client was not the owner of the store. He was acting as a retail consultant, primarily in working out financial operations, as well as coordinating the entire effort of starting the new enterprise. So I was essentially working through a middleman.

We all first met at the owner's house, where I was to present my preliminary design scheme. Steve, the retail consultant, had

FIGURE 9-10
View of centralized sales desk of the Pages For All Ages bookstore from the main entry. Painted gypsum board and steel stud openings serve to unify the displays and integrate all of the architectural elements. Design and drawing by Andy Pressman.

FIGURE 9-11

The pinwheel layout of the store (above) and lighting and ceiling design (below) are intended to provide visual excitement and drama. Display quadrants are organized around the sales desk. Design and drawings by Andy Pressman.

Bay Windows

Platform

Entry

Sales Desk

Staff Desk

Island Fixtures

Info Desk

Office

Receiving & Stock

Wall Fixtures

Floor Plan

Lay-in Fluorescent Lighting

Indirect Lighting

Soffits

Lower Ceiling

Higher Ceiling

Ceiling Plan

provided me with requirements for the store, and I had created a design without a dialogue with the owners. Everyone, however, seemed to like and approve the design, including the always unconditionally supportive Isaac.

The big departure in terms of design was an emphasis on three-dimensional forms, rather than on costly finishes. The forms—built from gypsum board and steel studs—would impart a unique identity and hopefully promote exploration through every square inch of the 6000 square-foot area. The idea was to use common materials in an uncommon way, and break the conventions of the typical right-angled box. The experience of browsing was intended to be dynamic, and change with every repeat visit.

Problems manifested themselves subsequent to completion of final construction documents. The events, unfortunately, were never clear to me: The owners were so upset that they simply refused to talk. It was their apparently irreconcilable differences with Steve that spilled-over to my work. I had no control—I was powerless to do anything to help correct any misperceptions. My sense from Steve was that the overarching issue was cost, and a contractor who undermined my design and documents. I could neither explain nor defend my position.

This was, by a considerable amount, the most frustrating project I have ever encountered. I felt that the design was noteworthy, and was quite proud of my work. The project was built (I've heard that much of the design was not followed), and the owners would not allow me to photograph it. I could not bring myself to take the three-hour drive to see the aborted work, and to confront the owners. To this day, when I see similar design elements in other buildings, I have momentary flashbacks, and picture my own project in its built reality. At least I maintain a good and ongoing professional relationship with Steve, who has since referred work to me. However, I now contract directly with the owners. You can't even *begin* to be a good politician if there is no personal relationship with your client.

CHAPTER 10

AN ACADEMIC PERSPECTIVE ON ARCHITECTS AND CLIENTS

In a recent *Wall Street Journal* article, Frederick Klein observed that many architects consider themselves "the Rodney Danger-fields of the nation's professionals: They don't get no respect." Then there is the story (told in an AIA Chicago publication) of Al Rosen, a young architect with a new firm in 1944, being escorted out of his Loop office for lunch by his Uncle Joe who said, "See that man over there," pointing to the most forlorn of Van Buren Street derelicts, "he's a retired architect." Is this bleak picture a self-fulfilling prophecy—ultimately resulting in both unsatisfied clients and architects—or, as Barry LePatner has said, just a bad public image of a profession in need of recognition of its role in today's society?

LePatner underscored the problem in an essay in *Architectural Record:* "Despite the apparent fascination with architecture, however, the public's image of architects remains two-dimensional. Without a true understanding of the many skills and qualities needed to orchestrate a successful project, those who retain architects can never fully appreciate the multifaceted talents an architect must possess."

This condition was further delineated in a 1993 survey conducted by The Roper Organization for the American Institute of Architects, which concluded that there are indeed gaps in clients' awareness of architects' expertise. Moreover, almost two-thirds of the institutional and business client respondents indicated that they thought architects were at least "somewhat arrogant," "elitist," and "demanding." [The goal of the research was to advise architects on how to improve marketing and project delivery services.]

In the present chapter, John Seiler of the Harvard University Graduate School of Design summarizes the current state of confusion in the profession, and architects' decreasing influence and power in the design and construction of buildings. A subsequent selection presents surprising results of a small pilot study that attempts to illuminate some of the problems noted above by comparing the professional–client relationship in architecture to that in the other great professions, law and medicine.

Debate about the Architect's Role—Future and Present [1]

John Seiler is an Adjunct Professor of Architecture and Urban Design at the Harvard University Graduate School of Design. He is an architect who consults with design firms on management issues and with schools on campus planning. Professor Seiler's publications include a contribution to The Instructor's Guide for the AIA Professional Practice Handbook *(1988),* "Architecture at Work" *in the* Harvard Business Review *(1984), and* Systems Analysis in Organizational Behavior *(Irwin, 1967).*

As worldwide economic ill health and a dilatory recovery continue to preoccupy many architects as they consider the state of their profession, this hopefully temporary condition tends to overshadow a more fundamental concern: Architects' diminishing influence over design and construction decisions. The struggle for power between architects and other construction industry role players is an increasingly menacing problem. More recently, the matter of project control has been further complicated by the growing industry practice of dividing responsibility among several firms for those elements of the design domain over which architects still are thought to preside.

---

1. © 1994 by the President and Fellows of Harvard College.

What jurisdictions have architects lost? If one compares the present situation with that of the so-called master builder of Medieval times, the losses are impressive, including the several varieties of engineering, construction, materials manufacture and supply, landscape architecture, facility and space planning, specialized programming, interior design, and, especially, alternative forms of client representation. Lest the comparison with a professional operating several centuries ago seem to trivialize this list of losses, note that, except for the first three categories, these losses have all taken place within this century and several within a matter of decades.

It is unlikely that anyone would argue that today's technological, political, organizational, economic, and other complexities make a return to the master builder form of project management possible, or even desirable. However, an argument can be made that the continuing disintegration of the role of the architect, particularly in the loss of full responsibility and authority to act as the chief agent for the client, has a greater price tag than a decline in the profession's esteem. More at stake is the exercise of qualified judgment, based not simply on aesthetic values, but on characteristics such as an organic sense of the project as a whole, responsiveness to potential future conditions, long-term competition for scarce resources, environmental quality, a broad definition of the "user" in both temporal and spatial terms, and other considerations commonly thought of as "in the public interest."

There are counterarguments, of course. Even if the consequences of disintegration of the architect's role were as stated, how many architects are prepared and willing to bring the cited perspectives to their projects, even in those shrinking numbers of cases where an architect is able to play a relatively traditional role? What is more, who says the architect is the only one suited to the integrative, multivalue task, even if there are architects who do practice that way?

As to the first question, possibly too few architects actually do take the "Olympian" view to which the above consequences refer. However, that admission need not lead to resignation. Instead, it could fuel a search for ways to increase the incidence and quality of architects' project leadership.

The second question, whether other role players could provide the needed perspective, is more complex. Part of the answer would have to confront another question: Is there a discipline inherent in architectural training and in standards of professional conduct that distinguishes architects from other potential construction project leaders as protectors of the public good? Objective, affirmative arguments are hard to find. Debate on this matter took place recently in Britain. In England, many in a position to influence legislation contended that British architects are no longer preeminent in the building team and do not deserve protection of the title, "architect," through statutory registration. Such protection, they argued, gives architects an unfair advantage over others in the construction industry. As a result of their arguments, British architects no longer enjoy the statutory protection of their title.

Some of the departures from traditional practice that may have given ammunition to British critics of architect protection have received considerable press in recent years. The "façade architect," presumably a decorative specialist, invariably also a "signature" or celebrated architect, is a preeminent example of the retreat of some highly visible architects from the traditional project leadership role. Their professional choice supports those who argue that architects lack interest in or denigrate the role of integrator and, therefore, forfeit any special privilege based on protection of the public good.

Less dramatic examples of architect specialization involve consultancies by well-known architects on commissions of lesser known architects. For example, a design office may carry a project only through the conceptual phase, or perhaps beyond into design development, then hand the products of that design work off to another architectural firm for development of contract documents and for site supervision. These cases of project splitting may be defended by a perceived need for knowledge about local conditions in the final stages of design. But some offices have developed reputations for expertise in their chosen stages of the design process. In either case, they appear to demonstrate that a single, integrative leader is not a requirement for good architecture.

A special case of dividing work among two or more architects is called "bridging," the product of two men's organizational innovation, George Heery of The Brookwood Group, and Charles Thomsen of 3/DI. Their project methodology is motivated, first, by the desire to achieve, early in the project, a guaranteed construction cost for the security of the owner. Their second goal is avoidance of liability claims on the part of the design architect, called in this system the "client's consultant." The owner hires the consultant to prepare a request for bid for "final engineering" (development of construction documents) and for construction of the project. The request for bid includes what may be considered on more traditional building projects to be fully detailed design development documents, including extensive specifications. Bidders consist of design-build organizations with the capability of assuming the role of "architect of record."

A simpler, perhaps precursor version of bridging is the role of the construction manager (CM), an agent of the client who may come on the scene at the feasibility phase of the project, or even earlier. The CM typically assists in feasibility studies, arranges for or provides programming services, manages architect and other specialist selections, provides overall management of the project, and, on occasion, may arrange for or provide facility management services to the owner, long-term.

When the evolution of the role of the architect in the construction industry and the consequences for architectural careers are the subject of discussion, the conversation often takes one of the following directions:

DIRECTION ONE

Since so many architecturally trained people are unemployed or underemployed in architecture, ways need to be found by which these people can achieve professional rewards outside of the field of architecture. The presumption is that architectural training is effective preparation for careers other than in traditional building design. It is not clear just what it is about architectural training that makes it useful elsewhere, or just where elsewhere is. In fact, a report titled, "Alternative Careers of Architectural Graduates," by Roger Schluntz, published in CRIT/ASJ in the Fall of 1980, describes the results of a survey of architectural graduates conducted by the Association of Collegiate Schools of Architecture in 1977. While noting possible methodological problems in the study, the following conclusion was drawn: "Other than the various areas in construction and real estate development, the frequency of the responses does not support any conclusion suggesting that the study of architecture provides a meaningful education appropriate to other areas of endeavor."

DIRECTION TWO
Architects must regain the leadership role in the construction process because only those in that role have the ability to understand and integrate all the values to which a project must respond.

The journal, *Progressive Architecture,* has published a series called "Architects and Power" (issues of 2/92, 5/92, 3/93, 6/93, and 9/93 contain these articles). Thomas Fisher, Executive Editor of the magazine, drew a parallel between architecture and the practice of law in an opening article. When lawyers became more plentiful than the demand for legal work, he reported, law education was redefined from simply preparation for practicing law to "a particular way of thinking." This reconception led many legally trained people into business and government where legal training was needed. Fisher sees society's need for solving many social ills as requiring "the sort of generalist, cross-disciplinary approach to problems that pervades almost everything architects do....If this profession is to survive as more than a shadow of its former self, we must begin to see ourselves as capable of offering a type of problem-solving rather than simply a type of design service." In his view, architecture, like other professions, suffers from "myopic specialization," which has hurt not only the profession but the public that it is supposed to serve.

Robert Gutman, a member of the Princeton architecture faculty, contributed to this series. He deplored the trend among architects to justify their role on grounds of technical expertise rather than artistic accomplishment. He pointed out that, in so doing, architects compete with many other professions that are more capable of delivering technology than are architects. He was puzzled by architects' neglect of that aspect of their profession that makes it "the mother of all arts." He suspected the reason is that architects fear that being identified with the arts will create the impression that their services are a luxury.

Historically, architecture has indeed been a luxury, Gutman observed. So, his solution was to cut back on the number of architects, architectural firms, and architecture graduates. He viewed as tragic the many "dedicated, talented men and women who are never able to realize the hopes and ambitions which drew them to the field." Furthermore, he contended that architecture schools have not begun to address this problem. He speculated that the solution will be found in encouragement of architecture graduates to "consider ties to allied fields."

Weld Coxe and Mary Hayden came to a very different conclusion, in a succeeding issue of *Progressive Architecture*. They found that "architects in private practice who provide more complete services to their clients seem without exception to be stronger, more influential, and more prosperous than their peers who take a less responsible role...[and] a large majority of the architects recognized as best in design...insist on taking the greatest responsibility for the complete execution of their work."

In Spain, where these authors found architects to be more highly regarded than doctors, accountants, and engineers, and possibly equal to lawyers, architectural education includes training in civil engineering. Spanish architects stamp all of a project's drawings, including those prepared by consulting engineers. One Spanish architect is quoted as saying, "Spanish architects have both technical and humanistic strengths." The article concluded with a question: "Is it time to move toward a new order of architectural practice in the United States—one in which responsibility is recognized as on a par with professionalism and creativity?"

(In interesting contrast, an essay titled, "Critical Differences," by David R. Scheer, appearing in Issue 1 of *Practices*, Spring 1992, compared building practices in France and the United States. In France, this author reported, the architect is primarily responsible, by statute, for representing cultural values on a project, and has relatively little technical function. The latter falls to engineers, contractors, and certain government agencies. For example, French architects do not prepare construction documents but do play an instrumental role in selecting the trade contractors who do prepare working drawings from the architect's design development documents and the architect must approve those working drawings. French architects, this article contended, are less conflicted than American architects, who are responsible for both a client's financial interests and interests of the public welfare. From these data French architects appear to be in a more secure position professionally than their United States counterparts.)

Sharon Sutton, professor at the University of Michigan, took a view in another of *Progressive Architecture's* articles on power that may complement that of Coxe and Hayden. She blamed architecture's plight on its lack of an information base. She drew a distinction between architecture as a profession that relates to a client's needs and architecture as a discipline that relates to a collective body of knowledge about the field. Developing that knowledge has been neglected, she insisted. She focused on "the interconnectedness of knowledge and the interdisciplinary character of all real-world problems." She quoted others with whom she shared criticism of "the 'spotlight' fixed on the design studio...[which] allows a sharp focus on the aesthetic and geometric dimensions, and blurred vision on the surrounding components." She blames this focus for deemphasizing critical thinking and writing and for the unwillingness of architects to "recognize research as a rigorous enterprise...[by example of the studio] where even the most casual inquiry qualifies as 'research.' "

Sutton proposed a two-track architectural training system, one for practitioners and the other for "a career in scholarship." She expected training in practice to benefit from scholarship and predicted architects would begin "looking outward to the disempowered, ...[focus on] the earth's ravaged resources, ...acknowledging our complicity, as a privileged group, in many of the inequities, ...articulating a moral purpose...[and to] make the built environment better for more of the earth's peoples."

And so goes the debate—not whether careers in architecture in America are in trouble, but what to do about the declining role of the profession. Carl Sapers, who was good enough to react to an earlier version of this note, suggested that the answer lies in a combination of changes—in regulations, in standards established and promulgated by the AIA, and in architectural education. Regarding regulations, for example, Sapers favored requiring a registered architect to be on the project during construction. A guideline to this effect has been adopted by the National Council of Architectural Registration Boards, he reported.

Among the steps the AIA might take would be an effort to rectify "the ignorance prominent architects display about questions of the economics of running an architectural firm." Sapers would not "pump for more practice courses," but he did feel that schools should "have rigorous requirements that the graduate understand a great deal more about the political and economic dynamics of practice."

A Jarring Footnote: The Need to Formally Explore the Architect–Client Relationship

The pitfall in carefully accumulating the thoughts and experiences of the best and the brightest lies in the tendency to generalize from this material; to conclude that it represents the entire panorama. In a conscious effort to frame the excellence of contributors' material to The Fountainheadache *with a broader perspective, I undertook a small pilot project that begins to look at the less than excellent underpinnings of architect–client relationships today.*

Introduction

The Fountainheadache notwithstanding, there is much evidence that the architect–client relationship is understudied, underdiscussed, and underrated. When this relationship has been specifically studied, it is either assessed by using static measures that focus on client satisfaction and perceptions of various publics, or it has been an issue subservient to the brilliant but global evocations of Judith Blau and Dana Cuff. Surprisingly little formal attention has been paid to the importance of the architect–client relationship from the point of view of architects. This condition appears to be in marked contrast to that of the other great professions, law and medicine, in which conventional wisdom holds that the intense and well-defined bond between practitioner and client transcends social, economic, and technical forces that have otherwise changed the face of practice. It is unlikely that there is a medical school in the United States that does not have a *sequence* of courses and clinical exercises devoted to the importance of establishing and maintaining rapport with patients.

In the context of heated debate about the role of architects and architecture, and in view of the now climactic confusion about resolving art, business, service, and preparation for the profession, it seems timely to explore what may hold potential for an increasingly important aspect of architectural life: The relationship between architect and client.

Background

Hugh Hardy has said that to get itself made, "Architecture has to be commerce." This accurate statement is an uncomfortable epitaph for a profession that once claimed parity with medicine, law, the ministry, and teaching. Robert Gutman's critical analysis of architectural practice is almost entirely focused on an elaboration of economic challenges to the integrity of practice. In summarizing the findings of a Canadian study, Kathryn Reid has reported that most respondents seemed more concerned about realizing a project and paid little attention to client needs or what were termed environmental conditions. In contrast to the grand service ideals of the Modern Movement, and compared with the tradition of the client- or patient-centered practice of law and medicine, *architecture is absolutely impoverished*. And operationalizing a recipe for the restoration of the health of the architectural profession seems considerably more difficult than rediscovering and enshrining noble roots.

Architecture is presently a field in which economic realities alone are potentially devastating. Lifetime earnings of practitioners and firms are substantially lower than their counterparts in law and medicine. Gutman observed that nearly half of the New York City offices that Blau interviewed for her study in 1974 were no longer in business in 1979. It is tempting to speculate that the pressure of fundamental economic survival may constitute an intervening variable that accounts for a significant measure of architects' focus on outcome (i.e., realizing the project), as a determinant of success and satisfaction (as opposed to the quality of the relationship with, or service to the client). The huge (in scope and scale) and the artistic bring financial reward and this may be reflected in the way young architects are trained and encultured. At a recent Harvard GSD roundtable, Curtis Davis commented that an ability to tap and manage data combined with a sensitivity to the needs of people are skills that are not being taught. Dana Cuff has stressed the need for broadening the vision and abilities of young architects, and for learning to function in a more collaborative, socially realistic setting.

While undoubtedly making important recommendations, Cuff and others have not considered the problems, ramifications, and potentials in the architect's *relationship with the client*. One informant in Blau's landmark study of architectural practice remarked that the most exciting work came about as a result of "continuous interaction" with an individual or business client. In a recent poll of readers of one of the major architectural journals, a large majority of respondents stated that they believed that successful client relationships were a matter of "chemistry," or having rapport with the client. As implied by the term "chemistry," and as indicated by Davis (previous page), development of rapport with those we serve appears to be elusive and undertaught despite some underlying awareness of its significance.

The relationship with the client as one manifestation of the zeal to serve others—the classical dedication of the professional to a calling—is a quality we may have come to largely neglect (despite the work of some of the extraordinary professionals recruited for *The Fountainheadache*). Two recent and large surveys of architecture clients conducted by the RIBA and the AIA, respectively, characterized architects as "arrogant." The British respondents viewed architecture overwhelmingly as a business and not as a profession.

Another startling development from Great Britain is the movement to abolish architect's registration. This is a proposal that has been likened to dismantling the National Council of Architectural Registration Boards in the United States, a move that, at the very least, undermines the credibility of the profession. It is just this sort of action that lends sobering credibility to the polemic analyses of Sharon Sutton, who seizes every opportunity to describe architects as impotent artisans and servants of venture capitalists. In the Canadian study (noted above) there was a virtually unanimous sentiment from clients that architects appear insensitive to client needs, particularly where functional requirements had what was seen as an adverse impact on aesthetics. The extent to which architect is estranged from client seems jarring.

Collectively, disturbing observations such as these just noted may simultaneously and paradoxically suggest a ray of hope in terms of improved efficacy and professional satisfaction for architects. F. I. Steele calls upon all architects to face up to impaired relations with those we are mandated to serve by invoking "organization theory," which sees the interpersonal process as a collection of variables that can be influenced as a function of our ability to face and analyze the problems. We may not be in a position to control economic pressure, but there are some forces we can influence. Again, however, there is the daunting task of identifying and translating the relevant social theory for architects and architecture today.

In a review essay on dyadic relations in a wider social context, Martha O'Mara outlined work that demonstrated how the character of interaction between individuals is determined by the larger social milieu. Seen in these terms, the impact of a group, a collective self-definition and perhaps even basic self-esteem helps to generate opinions and standards among the members of a given dyad (i.e., an architect and client). While this dyad may defy the clean calculus of social exchange theory, the notion of "secondary" exchange (as delineated by O'Mara) may be illuminating. One may see personal relationship mediated by norms that have been perpetuated by some larger institution, such as a professional subculture. It may be argued that a change or derangement of the subculture, regardless of the cause, may flavor the expectations and direction of interactions between individuals. If the subculture of architecture places an exclusively high value or "social approval" upon making built objects, then the reward for achieving that outcome may be sufficiently compelling to outweigh the reward derived from service to individual clients.

The small pilot study I recently undertook probes the status and import of the architect–client relationship by looking at a subset of professionals who may be predisposed to, and situated in a position that allows gratification from provision of service (i.e., from *process* in contrast to *outcome)*. This subset is comprised by the practitioner with a small scale practice, one who is likely to be a sole proprietor. In view of the sociology that defined the relatively intimate relationships of the rural and small scale society as compared with the impersonal economic relationships of the city, it would appear that an exploration of the place and nature of relationships with clients among small scale practitioners would be illuminating. It seems unlikely that this group of professional is "in it for the money."

Objectives

The goal of my inquiry was to conduct a pilot evaluation of the general hypothesis that architects currently in small scale general practice derive a significant degree of satisfaction from the evolving relationship with the client, and that sources of professional satisfaction among architects engaged in small scale practice will parallel sources of satisfaction among lawyers and physicians similarly engaged. In gross statistical terms then, the hypothesis is that there would be little or no difference between the three groups of professionals on the dimensions of the dependent variable (delineating quality of, and gratification from an evolving relationship with the client or patient).

Methods

(I) SUBJECTS

The subjects ($n=15$) are five architects, five lawyers, and five physicians drawn from referral lists generated by their respective professional associations. The criterion for inclusion in the study was involvement in small scale practice. The Boston Society of Architects prepared a listing of AIA members in Massachusetts who provide architectural services for residential and small scale commercial projects, and who are capable of working on those projects for which the total design and construction budget is under 300,000 dollars. The Boston Bar Association provided a listing of their members who concurrently belong to the solo and small firm task force. And finally, the Massachusetts Chapter of the American Academy of Family Physicians (in Manchester, MA) provided a listing of those family physicians who are engaged in solo or small group practice.

Subjects in all groups were recruited only with the understanding that they were participating in a study about sources of professional satisfaction, the dependent variables. In addition to the principal independent variable, small scale practice, other independent variables include age, gender, income range, average elapsed time in practice, and nature of practice.

(II) PROCEDURE

All subjects were assessed with a survey instrument and semi-structured interview designed to probe dimensions of professional satisfaction addressed by the hypothesis. The two modes of eliciting data provided some degree of convergent validity, though the small sample size is clearly the most serious threat to validity in this pilot study. A "survey instrument" and a partially designed interview served more as a means of organizing rather than eliciting data. The basic method of inquiry here was fundamentally that of case study. In an exploratory probe of the sort represented by the present study, a case series of five subjects within the group in question and in two comparison groups seems most appropriate.

Subjects were asked to base their responses to questions on their experiences and feelings during the previous six months. Ratings for the survey were made on a five-point rating scale on which each scale point was labeled to reflect the degree to which the subject agrees with some statement about practitioner–

client/patient relationships. The survey is intended to facilitate preliminary statistical characterization and comparison of the groups, and pilot a test of the hypothesis.

Standard interview questions included probes into the following areas: (1) general flavor of practice and typical client/patient; (2) ability to resolve conflicts with clients/patients; (3) degree to which relationships with clients/patients have been gratifying; (4) degree to which outcomes (built project, legal action, medical improvement) have been gratifying.

Results and Discussion

The major finding of this pilot study was that the trend among architects, in contrast to that among physicians and lawyers, is that architects derive the greater part of their professional satisfaction from outcome and *not* process. As a central element of "process," the give and take between professional and client seems little more than that which must be tolerated by the architects studied in this sample. Moreover, outcome is described by the architects studied in terms of the degree to which they feel that their *built* work is of artistic/aesthetic quality as defined both by their personal vision and by prevailing architectural sentiment.

In sharp contrast, satisfaction among physicians and lawyers appears to develop more readily as a result of the ongoing activities involved in serving the needs of their clients/patients. Therefore, outcome is relegated to the "icing on the cake," as one respondent put it.

The data, therefore, failed to support the original hypothesis. The preliminary data here may suggest that sources of professional satisfaction are roughly the same for comparable subsets of lawyers and physicians, and very different for architects.

The architects studied tend to be at best ambivalent about providing services to clients. Relationships with clients are seen as epiphenomenal, and there may even be something approaching pride taken in the case of an estranged relationship.

Lawyers and physicians cite interpersonal relations with a "sophisticated" client/patient as the most desirable and fulfilling aspect of their work. What is intriguing about these professionals is that they seem very happy with all aspects of day-to-day routines. Typical client/patient problems are not resolved quickly; there is generally no great concrete and steel outcome. So what keeps these folks "in there?" It seems, in listening to the discussions, that it is the process—the helping, and the relationship that develops coincident with that process. As Richard Selzer has said, it is the almost religious quality of the bond that develops between the patient and the one who is attending to the patient.

The essence of professional life for this sample of lawyers and doctors is taking care of people. The architects are not taking care of people; rather, they are focusing exclusively on creating a beautiful built object. If this observation is demonstrated to be valid and generalizable, the appealing question then becomes, how do we reacquaint architects with the tradition of serving people? Certainly, we cannot relieve the severe economic pressures (though economic forces are not manifestly reflected in the interview material). Social–psychological, educational, and enculturation forces are the variables we *can* modify.

Architects did not enjoy mundane aspects of practice nearly as much as the other two groups of professionals, they rated praise from colleagues as more important than did the other groups, and felt (as did the lawyers) that clients should have personality styles similar to their own. One interpretation of these results is that architects found it easier or less threatening to reveal ambivalence about relationships with clients in the course of an interview. Another possible explanation is that the survey question designed to specifically probe relationships with clients was poorly constructed (in an untested survey instrument, this risk is always present). It may also be that there are aspects of mundane practice, of "process," other than client relationships that are significantly aversive for the architects, and this should be explored in future research. Nevertheless, the interview data on architects' views on their relationships with clients remain as compelling material that must also be studied further in subsequent and expanded investigation. Additional evaluation of the impact of the lower income level for architects seems worthy of attention.

The long-term results of broadening the present study in the future will likely yield a detailed accounting of the foundations of professional satisfaction for today's young architects. In so doing, it is hoped that meaningful new recommendations for architectural education in the realm of professional practice and the design studio can be actively defined, developed, and ultimately tested.

Bibliography

1. American Institute of Architects. "Clients Polled: What They Think Can Help You Market." *Memo.* November 1993, 4–5.

2. Askew, Lee. "A Fresh Look at Ourselves." *Memo.* February 1993, 15.

3. Blau, Judith. *Architects and Firms: A Sociological Perspective on Architectural Practice.* Cambridge, MA: The MIT Press, 1984.

4. Cuff, Dana. *Architecture: The Story of Practice.* Cambridge, MA: The MIT Press, 1991.

5. Cuff, D. and E. Robertson. "Words and Images; the Alchemy of Communication." *Journal of Architectural Education.* 36, Winter 1982, 8–15.

6. Diamonstein, Barbaralee. *American Architecture Now.* New York: Rizzoli, 1980, 85.

7. Dietsch, Deborah. "Europe's New Conflict." *Architecture.* 82, September 1993, 15.

8. Disckind, Barbara. "Hiring an Architect: One Couple's Perspective." *AIA/DC News.* April 1993, 5.

9. Freiman, Ziva. "Reader Poll: Architect–Client Relations." *Progressive Architecture.* 71, February 1990, 63–65.

10. Greenstreet, Robert. "The Architect/Client Relationship." *Progressive Architecture.* 67, July 1986, 63.

11. Gutman, Robert. *Architectural Practice: A Critical View.* New York: Princeton Architectural Press, 1988.

12. Gutman, Robert. "Architecture: The Entrepreneurial Profession." *Progressive Architecture.* 58, May 1977, 55–58.

13. Harms, Hans. "User Involvement: Toward a New Professionalism." *RIBA Journal.* 81, February 1974, 26–29.

14. LePatner, Barry B. "The Profitable Professional: It pays to Maintain Good Client Relationships." *Architectural Record.* 172, January 1984, 27–29.

15. McKee, Bradford. "Surveys Reveal Clients' Views of Architects." *Architecture.* 82, December 1993, 91.

16. O'Mara, Martha A. "Social Processes: Dyadic Relations in a Social Context." *Unpublished Manuscript,* 1987.

17. Pawley, Martin. *Theory and Design in the Second Machine Age.* Oxford, England: Basil Blackwell, 1990.

18. Pawley, Martin. "The Case for Uncreative Architecture." *Architectural Record.* December 1992, 20.

19. Probst, Dorothy. "What the AIA Can Do for Me: Thoughts on AIA Leadership in the Marketplace." *CCAIA Focus.* July/August 1992, 7.

20. Rapoport, Amos. "Science and the Failure of Architecture: An Intellectual History." *Human Behavior and Environment Advances in Theory and Research.* 11, 1990, 79–109.

21. Reid, Kathryn. "The Presentable Architect." *The Canadian Architect.* 33, April 1988, 42–43.

22. "Risky Relationships: Are Your Good Client Relationships One-to-One or Firm-to-Firm?" *A/E Marketing Journal.* 15, March 1983, 2.

23. Robbins, Edward. "The Client in Architectural Education: Three Interviews at M.I.T." *Journal of Architectural Education.* 35, Fall 1981, 32–35.

24. The Roper Organization and The Gorman Group. *What Clients Need.* Washington, DC: The American Institute of Architects, 1993.

25. Salmon, Karen. "Interiors Committee Debates Value of Design." *Architecture.* June 1992, 28.

26. Saunders, William. "Roundtable Discussions on Designers' Power and Influence." *GSD News.* Fall 1993, 7.

27. Seiler, John. "Debate about the Architect's Role—Future and Present." *The President and Fellows of Harvard College,* 1993.

28. Selzer, Richard. *Mortal Lessons: Notes on the Art of Surgery.* New York: Simon and Schuster, 1976, 48.

29. Steele, F. I. "Interpersonal Aspects of the Architect–Client Relationship." *Progressive Architecture.* 49, March 1968, 132–133.

30. Sutton, Sharon. "The Progress of Architecture." Progressive Architecture. 74, October 1993, 76–79.

31. Tatum, Michael. "Hot Buttons and Cosmic Visions." *Architectural Record.* August 1992, 32.

32. Tönnies, Ferdinand. *Gemeinschaft and Gesellschaft.* (1887). Translated and edited by C.P. Loomis as *Community and Society.* New York: Harper & Row, 1963.

33. Waters, Brian. "Context: What the Client Wants from Us." *Architects' Journal.* 170, November 14, 1979, 1047–1050.

INDEX